Ten Thousand Campfires

Ten Thousand Campfires

REX ELLIS

First published in 2005 by Central Queensland University Press

Second published in 2012 by Boolarong Press, Salisbury, Brisbane, Australia.

National Library of Australia Cataloguing-in-Publication entry

Author:	Ellis, Rex, 1942-
Title:	Ten thousand campfires / Rex Ellis.
ISBN:	9781921920653 (pbk.)
Subjects:	Ellis, Rex, 1942-
	Safaris--Australia.
	Safaris--Africa.
	Safaris--India.
	Australia--Description and travel.
	Africa--Description and travel.
	India--Description and travel.
Dewey Number:	910.4092

Cover design and typesetting by Jane Dorrington

Cartoons courtesy George Aldridge

Printed and bound by Watson Ferguson and Company, Salisbury, Brisbane, Australia.

To my daughters

Georgi and Katherine

Foreword

A dry, almost invisible dust that became one with the windless air, giving pungency to its taste, bringing restlessness and energy to the blood.

(Vance Palmer, *The Swayne Family, 1934)*

The '*Spirit of Australia*' is a title that evokes a rich spectrum of varied images and sounds. Images such as the heroes of Gallipoli, those men and women who have handed down the legacy of national pride and sacrifice. Images of our sporting heroes who have raised the bar to a new level and positioned themselves in the sporting halls of fame. We glory in the term *digger*, we know the meaning of *mateship* and share a common and sentimental bias in favour of the *underdog*. Images of the bush for which many of us have a nostalgic yearning. Images of the beach and the sea which help define our identity both here and abroad. As a multicultural and diverse group of people, it is that and so much more that proudly makes us Australian.

But what of the great Australian hinterland described to us by eminent Australian writers? In 1905 Ernest Favenc wrote:

> *"There is a wondrous fascination to it, in its strange loneliness and the hidden mysteries it might contain. To pass a night alone in the desert spinifex country, is to feel as much cut off from the ordinary life of the world as one could feel if transplanted to another sphere ...." (Voices of the Desert)*

It is this imposing and mysterious Australian outback replete with stories, *the kind of stuff dreams are made of* that is an integral aspect of the Spirit of Australia and is the home of Rex Ellis. This is his land, his sensibility and it would be formidable to nominate any of its vast deserts, its ancient mountain ranges and dried up creek beds that have not been traversed or surveyed by him.

In his new book, *Ten Thousand Campfires,* he tells many anecdotal stories introducing us to the adventurers of the land he knows so well. I have had personal experience of travelling with Rex to those uninhabited and untenanted parts of Australia that were utterly inaccessible and remote to me. I shared many a campfire with him and heard a story or two during those journeys. He introduced me, as he has done for so many to the *Great Australian Loneliness* (in apologia to Ernestine Hill) and revealed its majesty, its solitude and kept faith with its mystery.

I have met many of those mentioned in the book. I have shared a campfire with Two-Mile Sheedy and been introduced to his Rain Dance. I can vouch for the stories about Murphy's mob, and when I reflect upon those years, I value greatly the memory of the day's end when Rex was the master of ceremonies, albeit censored, at times by Stoney and Bill.

Rex travels in the bush as an inveterate traditionalist. Those who read *Ten Thousand Campfires* will, I am sure, be drawn like moths to a light and share that part of the Spirit of Australia about which we often dream, and which has now been made reality by a great Australian.

The Honourable Justice Paul Guest, Q.C.

Introduction

This book is a 'camp oven stew' of experiences, including some from overseas. The common factor applying to most of them is that there was always a campfire, not too far away.

An inland Australian campfire is a very special thing, not the least because of its physical makeup. If the builders of the fire know their stuff, most fires will be burning some of the world's best hardwoods. After many years experience, I have found that the big three are Coolibah, (*Eucalyptus Microtheca*) Myall, (*Acacia Sowdenii*) and Gidgee (*Acacia Georginae and Cambagei*). If the timber is not rotten, it will supply coals for up to twenty-four hours after the fire has burnt down. This makes them good for cooking on and for sitting around on cold nights, as well as requiring less labour in the gathering of wood. I will dispense with the mechanics of selecting woods and building fires, before I become bogged down in technicalities.

I would like to dwell for a few paragraphs on the aesthetic and the spiritual aspects of the outback campfire. If you are not under your own roof, you are home where your fire is, with your swag close by. This has been the case since Europeans first landed in this country, and has always been the case with the Aborigines. There is no better way of getting to know people, than spending time around a campfire. A psychiatrist client of mine once told me, and I quote, "If I could swap my couch for a campfire, my patients would be far better off." Perhaps a few reds or rums would assist them even further.

If you are camped on your own, a campfire can be good company; If you are feeling miserable, then a campfire will cheer you up; when you are feeling cold, a campfire will keep you warm; and when you are hungry, the campfire will cook your food.

A campfire should be well managed on all occasions, by only burning the necessary wood. Cooking on a campfire is a bushman's art, but many good cooks are not necessarily good fire managers. What coals, ash and flame are available must be used to provide a multi-course meal for a mob of people, ideally without losing your eyebrows, or ending up with part of the meal still cold, or half of your burnt wood in the rest of it. A huge number of people have no idea of how to boil a billy properly to make a brew of tea, but I won't get into that here.

Sadly, for a large proportion of the population, the campfire is becoming an endangered 'species'. For the most part, and increasingly so, the majority of the public who travel outback, are pretty well 'yarded up' in caravan parks and dedicated camping areas. They sit in plastic chairs, trying to appear cheerful, around a bewildering array of portable gas stoves. Many of these regulations are necessary, but I fear that there is a whole generation of Aussies growing up, who won't ever have a fair dinkum campfire experience; not good.

My final observation on this subject, concerns the treatment of the campfire when it has been finished with, and bear in mind, I'm talking particularly about fires in the desert or semi desert areas, where bushfires don't pose a potential problem. The authorities will advise people to put water on it or to bury it. In many cases people don't have water to spare, or don't carry the proper shovel with them, even if they do know how to dig a decent hole; and invariably the ground is too hard to dig. The best method is to simply spread the ashes, using a long-handled shovel or a branch, avoiding other flammable material. This means that, after the next rain, the evidence of your fire is all but eliminated; a stark contrast from heaps of unsightly ash, often surrounded by stones. Anyway, this is not a 'Boys Own' camping manual, so I'll get back to the main theme. My last word on this subject is simply this: you can't have a fair dinkum outback experience without a campfire, even if it's not every night.

Contents

1. A Bungled Billy Boil

In my second year of operation in the safari business, I was heading out to the Nullarbor on a twelve-day safari. My vehicle for this adventure was a Land Rover station wagon, and my party comprised three Melbourne ladies and a couple of blokes from New South Wales, one of whom was a dentist, the other a postman.

Our first night's camp was in Mulga country near Kingoonya, on the Trans Australia Railway. Once I had lit the fire, it used to be my habit to set up a couple of card tables and to put out the fold up chairs. I would then put out a flagon of red wine, and a flagon of white wine, before commencing to prepare the evening meal. As soon as the blokes had sunk a couple of reds, they began to argue. This was no friendly argument either, and the ladies appeared to get quite uncomfortable and embarrassed. Meanwhile, I was around the back of the wagon in my kitchen, wondering what on earth I was going to do about this situation. I had not long been in the business of carting people around the scrub, so I was at a complete loss.

Next day, as I negotiated the wheel tracks that ran alongside the transcontinental line, I was preoccupied with this problem. While travelling through the day, the men wouldn't converse, and I always ensured that they had a lady in the middle of the rear seat. Always the optimist, I thought that the first night's incident was a one-off happening. This however was not to be.

The second evening's camp was a carbon copy of the previous night; the argument starting soon after the happy hour had begun, and I noted that the dentist and the postman were the main offenders. Another uncomfortable evening was endured, and as I lay in my swag, contemplating the situation, I came to the conclusion that I would have to somehow short circuit this predicament; somehow I didn't think that talking to them would solve anything. Nothing can be done in these situations, without the rest of the party being privy to it. Finally, I drifted off into a troubled sleep, no closer to the solution to this crisis.

Around mid morning the next day, as we were grinding through the sand dunes near the railway line (there was no road there in those days), it suddenly came to me what I should do about this tight spot. It was a radical idea but I figured that the circumstances warranted my decision. Our third campsite, once more near the railway line, was in Mallee and spinifex country, with the railway actually providing us with an ongoing floorshow. There were various freight trains passing, and the Transcontinental Express hurried by. Without fail, the drivers (I knew several of them) would give us a wave, and sound a blast of the horns on their locomotives; it was a novelty for them to see a vehicle, out in this remote part of the Great Victoria Desert.

On this particular night, I set up the camp with a real purpose, paying particular attention to how I built my fire. I assembled it in a fashion often employed by Boy Scouts and Girl Guides, building it up about fifteen centimetres high, and on this platform, I placed a billy of water; I then lit the fire. The grog had been out for about twenty minutes, and sure enough, the arguments were starting to warm up. The women looked totally lost, and I thought that what I was about to do, would take their minds off the protagonists.

I went around to the back of the Land Rover and poured myself a pannikin of Pirramimma vintage wine, mainly to give myself a few revs, while I waited for the billy to boil, and for the arguments to reach a fever pitch. When I judged the moment to be just right, I psyched myself up, let forth a great bellow, and spun out from the back of the Rover. I lined up the boiling billy and rushed towards it, preparing myself for the greatest place kick ever seen. The resultant sight was pure poetry in motion, as I rushed at the fire and gave the billy an almighty boot. It took off like a Blue Streak rocket, soaring through the air and turning over several times, before spilling its boiling contents onto the spinifex, some nine or ten metres away. I then stopped, spun around and glared at the men who were, by this time, sitting bolt upright with their mouths wide open and their eyeballs protruding. At the top of my voice I yelled, “Bastards” and stalked off into the Mallee. I walked out of sight of the camp and sat down on a stump for about twenty minutes, contemplating what I had just done.

As I made my way slowly back to the camp, I observed the scene through gnarled and twisted branches of the Mallee trees. It was a ludicrous sight with every member of the party appearing very industrious, busy doing bugger all. The ladies were resetting the table, probably for the third or fourth time, while the blokes were just trying to appear busy. I reckoned they thought that I’d lost it, and they were particularly worried. I didn’t say

A Radical Solution

much, just put the billy back on the fire and served up the evening meal. When we'd finished, I told a few yarns, doing most of the talking for the rest of the night.

Later that evening, the dentist took me aside and actually apologised for his behaviour. He told me that he had never before been affected by anybody like that; but he agreed to be civil, as long as he was not made to sit next to his rival in the vehicle. The postman never did say anything; it takes all types to make a world.

Footnote:

On a trip in Northern Australia, some years later, we had two Land Rovers with a party of ten. A problem, very similar to that just described, made itself evident, with two blokes at loggerheads; and getting worse.

I said to my mate, "Don't you worry, I know just how to sort these blokes out!" Well! I did exactly what I had done before, setting the billy on a platform of sticks before lighting the fire. After my tot of Dutch courage, I rushed from behind the vehicle, and giving the best roar that I could dredge up, I lined up the billy for the kick of a lifetime, enthusiastically swinging my right boot forward. Unfortunately, I missed my target, and for a little while, I thought that my ankle was broken. I had driven my boot, full force, into the ground in front of the fire, tipping the billy over and extinguishing the fire. The whole camp erupted in laughter, and when everyone had settled down, I told them the whole story about my previous experience. This, fortunately, had the desired effect anyway, but it was a difficult way of going about it.

2.

Passing Twenty Cents

There are some things in life that you do, and get away with, more by good luck than good management, and this event is one of them. I was operating a boat trip down the Cooper Creek to Lake Eyre, in the record flood year of 1974. I had a party of five, as well my offsider and myself. The party included a lady by the name of Mary, who used to book to go on my most adventurous trips, including the first four wheel drive crossing of the Simpson Desert, and now this Cooper trip.

I have always found that, with some of the most disagreeable people, if you 'boundary ride' them enough times, you will eventually find a good side to them. However, this didn't seem to apply to Mary; I wore a trench around her trying to find one, but to no avail. I once asked her why she came on these trips, and her answer was, "to get away from the air-conditioning." She would bring her own supply of spirits, (Scotch) which she would drink in her swag before retiring. In the mornings, she would appear at the campfire, clad as always, in a leopard skin patterned jump suit, looking like an escapee from hell; she was a small, red-haired lady, who wore gold-rimmed glasses. I would ask, "How are you going Mary?" or similar, and her response was always a kind of grunt, that I took to mean 'ratshit' or something similar. Her breakfast consisted of as many cups of coffee as I was willing to give her. Now that I've painted such a dismal picture, I have to say that I had a grudging admiration for her. She was so physically weak, that I had to lift her into the boats every morning, but she didn't seem to have any fear of anything. The event I am about to describe, occurred at one of the most inaccessible places in Australia, the mouth of Cooper Creek. It was a very difficult and lengthy process to get a vehicle in there, and any medicals would have required a chopper.

My idea was to get a reaction out of Mary, that was all, so with that in mind, I decided to serve plum pudding for sweets that evening. There was no wood available for a fire, as there are no trees on the bottom end of Cooper Creek, so we had a Nitre bush fire. We used the dead roots of this tough shrub, a low, wide spreading bush, that is often the only perennial growing around salt lakes. It has an edible berry, much liked by Major Mitchell Cockatoos, but a Nitre bush fire is never very substantial. We were all sitting on our swags around the small fire, when I served up the pudding and tinned cream, and I slipped a twenty cent piece into Mary's pudding. As I said, my idea was to see how she would react; just a simple bit of human curiosity on my part. She was sitting on the opposite side of the fire to me, and I watched surreptitiously from under my hat as she ate her pudding. I saw every mouthful, and I watched, as she slowly worked her way through the pudding, expecting anytime for the coin to go 'clang', or whatever. Then, to my horror, I saw her scraping her plate. I knew empirically that she hadn't discovered it and pulled it out, and I was dead certain that she must have swallowed it.

When I was a young kid, I swallowed a sixpence, so my mother, who is a determined lady, eventually recovered it after some weeks of patient spadework; but a twenty cent piece? I didn't reckon it was possible for it to make the journey, and I was considering the possible consequences; I thought manslaughter might not be out of the question.

All that night, I lay in my swag, waiting for a scream in the darkness; I didn't get a minutes sleep. A couple of times, I went to Mary's camp and checked on her, but she appeared to be normal. Next morning, one of the best sights I had seen in years, was Mary as she wobbled over the small sand hillock, and I received the usual reply to my inquiry about how she slept, so I at least had a reprieve. All that day my mate, Brenton Ramsay and I, watched Mary like hawks, but we didn't see any unusual behaviour.

The next night I had a few hour's sleep, but still not a good night, and this went on for the next three days of the trip. As we motored down the east coast of Lake Eyre, Brenton wondered whether the Scotch might have dissolved the coin, but I didn't think that would be the case. No, I reckon she was a time bomb waiting to go off, and I was feeling for both of us.

Finally, the trip finished, and when I arrived home, I straightaway rang my old family doctor. I said something like, "Look, I know this lady that swallowed a twenty cent piece. Do you think she would be able to pass it?" He told me that she shouldn't have a problem passing it, and I was incredibly relieved. But then I did another very stupid thing, I phoned another doctor for a second opinion, and I was back to square one. He said that there was no way this lady could pass the offending coin, simply not possible.

By this time, I was sort of fatalistic about it, it was out of my hands. I heard from Mary from time to time, one occasion being a post card from Tanzania. I could only presume that the twenty cent piece was out of circulation for good, hopefully, a long way from Mary.

3.

The Mad American

I have been carrying people, from all walks of life, around the bush for thirty-nine years. Moreover, almost without exception, they are people that I would be very happy to meet again. Many have become good friends, however, during that time, I've met about thirty people that I wouldn't carry again, under any circumstances. I actually carry a little book with the letters, N.T.B.R. on the cover. These letters stand for *Never To Be Rebooked.* This chapter concerns two such people.

The incidents described here occurred on one of my Cape York safaris. I took my first party up there in 1969, and I've operated many very comprehensive trips since that, in the seventies and eighties. These safaris usually started in Cairns, and the vehicles would be driven up on a five-day service run from Adelaide, with some of the party travelling with us, and the rest meeting us in Cairns. These service runs were informal, enjoyable affairs involving a lot of driving, but with a lot of bush pubs and many other diversions along the way.

The two people in question, Ralph and his wife, were Americans, and Ralph was sixty years of age, a tall, raw-boned bloke who liked to roll his sleeves up, further than they were designed to go. He was an ex university professor, and his wife was twenty-five years his junior. I must make mention here that these are the only Americans in my little black book.

On the way up to Cairns on the service run, they gave me no indication that they might be a problem, although I couldn't help noticing that they liked their grog. Ralph had a peculiar habit of collecting bones, and whilst we powered along the track, all of a sudden, he would holler out "pull up", and we'd have to come to an abrupt halt. He would grab a string bag, jump out of the vehicle, and run back to some road kill that caught his eye, then souvenir a couple of bones, and come back to take his seat again. A number of string bags, full of assorted bones, already adorned my roof rack, and the collection was getting larger all the time. I thought that this was a bit unusual, but I didn't mind; people do have some strange interests.

On the way up to Cairns, we did experience a bit of drama that we could well have done without. There were three vehicles in our convoy, and mine was a new, D1310, two-ton, twin cab International; a heavy four wheel drive, with a covered-in loading area at the rear. The second vehicle, my older C1300, four wheel drive International, with a similar configuration, was being driven by Peter Coombe, while Peter Bosworth drove a Land Rover station wagon. At that time, CB radios were not available, so apart from hand signals, we had no reliable communication between the vehicles. I was travelling along this wheel-track road, through thick Mulga scrub, with a netting fence along the left-hand side. The Land Rover followed behind me, and the other Inter brought up the rear. As I drove out of the scrub, and up a rise into open Mitchell Grass country, a large road train confronted me, travelling fast, with a huge cloud of dust following behind. I quickly pulled off the track, and watched the semi roar past me. I doubted that the driver of the rig was even aware of my presence. I had grave fears for the welfare of the other two drivers, and I was unable to warn them of the approaching juggernaut. Peter Bosworth emerged from the Mulga, just in time to swerve off the track, but Peter Coombe in the other Inter, was too far back, avoiding the dust that we had raised. We turned our vehicles around, and headed back into the scrub, hot on the heels of the truck. After about a kilometre, we encountered our other truck, with its nose in a drain, up against the netting fence. It had a broken windscreen and a broken main leaf of the front, right-hand spring. The people in the truck were fairly shaken up, but fortunately, nobody had received any injuries. Ralph was more concerned about the fate of his bone collection.

Peter, who is a very good driver, had been travelling along the track, oblivious to the approaching road train, when it suddenly loomed up in front of him, leaving him very few options but to head for the drain. He yanked the wheel to the left, 'cutting a few posts', as the truck cut a swathe through a lot of light Mulga. He told us that it seemed to him like slow motion, as he watched the rear trailer of this monster drifting towards him, powerless to do anything. He said that it must have missed the rear of his truck by barely inches, just before he came to a shuddering stop in the drain. We reckoned that the truckie must have been on pills, and probably had no idea of the mayhem that he had caused. We clamped the spring, fitted a plastic windscreen, and continued on our way to Cairns. We stayed there for a day, sorting out our vehicles, and boxing our stores, in preparation for the twenty-one day Cape York safari.

All went well for a start, but on the second day, in the Laura area, as we were inspecting a gallery of Aboriginal paintings, Ralph managed somehow to close the Land Rover door on his thumb. For a supposedly tough bloke, he put on a hell of an act, and his wife said something about him being a haemophiliac. Anyway, I made a fuss of him, even forgoing a look at Percy Trezise's private collection of bark paintings, on display in the Laura pub. I took him back to our idyllic camp on the banks of the Laura River, and made him comfortable. "Whatever it takes" is my motto.

Next day we took off to the north, up the very badly corrugated phone line track, a track so bad, that it was impossible to exceed sixty kilometres per hour. It was full of huge bulldust holes, so we just rattled along and put up with it. Every half hour or so, I'd stop and wait until I could see Peter Coombe's dust, the normal thing to do pre CB radios. On one of these occasions, in the early afternoon, I was waiting on top of a rise, when I saw the Land Rover approaching, with its large dust cloud following. Peter Bosworth came to a halt and gave us the news, that the other Inter had lost a front wheel, just what I didn't want to hear. We drove back along the track for about four kilometres, before we came across the Inter, hard up against the bank, and sporting only three wheels. Peter said that he had been rattling along at about fifty kilometres per hour, when looking out of the window, he saw his front wheel running alongside. Like a wounded DC3, he nosed it into the soft bank on the side of the road, with no one any the worse for wear.

This was not a good situation, I thought, suddenly wishing that I was doing something else for a living. I decided then that I'd set up a base camp on the banks of the Hann River, little more than a kilometre or so to the south. Like most of the Cape York watercourses, this was a delightful place, with a gallery rain forest along each bank, with beautiful, crystal-clear water running swiftly by. This was my one piece of good fortune. A little later, I walked around to the back of the truck, where I noticed Ralph taking numerous stubbies of beer out of the fridge. I pointed out to him that the beer belonged to everyone, to which he took immediate offence. "What sort of an outfit is this? Losing a wheel and leaving us out in the bush." With that, he headed back to the river camp, still muttering under his breath. I had other things on my mind, however. It appeared that the excessive corrugations had caused a locking tab to break, thus allowing the castle nut to come off the end of the stub axle, leaving the wheel free to come off and career down the road. The stub axle had been wrecked, the whole axle housing had been twisted, and so a whole new front end was required.

We drove about fourteen kilometres into Hann River station, where the owner was extremely helpful. I was able to ring Percy Trezise, who was now back in Cairns, who offered to remove the rear seats from his Cessna, and to fly in a second hand front end, so that we could repair the 'International'. We headed back to the camp, to where the rest of the party was enjoying the enforced base camp on the edge of the Hann River. I was totally buggered, and I reckoned that I might have copped a touch of the sun, bending down through the heat of the afternoon. The boys talked me into lying down on my swag while they prepared our evening meal.

The river here was only about thirty metres wide, and I noticed that there was a small island in the middle. It was connected to the bank by the trunk of a fallen Iron Wood tree, so Ralph and his wife had quickly laid claim to it, setting up their swags upon it. Ralph had been complaining loudly, ever since we had returned from Hann River station, about our breakdown situation. He was definitely my second biggest problem, and he was drinking twice as much as anyone else.

All of a sudden, he jumped up, telling all and sundry that he was going to bed, and with that, he began to walk out across the log. He was about half way across when he started to get the wobbles, and with a startled "Goddamn", he fell into the river. I quickly brightened up and started to take an interest in proceedings. The depth of water at this point was only about sixty centimetres, but it was flowing quite swiftly, and Ralph started tumbling along like a praying mantis with a busted wing. Peter Bosworth sprang up and hurried over to the river in an attempt to pull Ralph out of the water. To my surprise, I called out, "let the bastard drown"; I knew that he wouldn't, but it must have been a nice thought, and I could see the rest of the party enjoying the spectacle. Peter was a very conscientious bloke so he went in and dragged Ralph out anyway. This bedraggled mess was a sad and sorry sight, cursing and spitting, but I knew that it was the highlight of my day. Being a natural optimist, I hoped that perhaps this might have a positive effect on his attitude, and maybe his behaviour would improve. That was, unfortunately, a forlorn wish.

Next day Percy Trezise flew in to Hann River Station with the replacement front end, which we had installed by mid afternoon. This achieved, we packed up our camp by the river, and headed north for a few hours, calling a halt when we reached Station Creek, just south of the little town of Coen.

The soup had just been served, and the two Peters and I were sitting on the tailgate of one of the 'Inters', enjoying a well-earned beer, when suddenly there was a torch shining in my face. It was Ralph and he exclaimed, "The brochure says that red and white table wines will be served with the evening meal, so where's the red wine?" Well! I couldn't believe my ears, and I called out, "Come here Ralph" and as he did, I reached behind me and grasped a jack handle. I really don't think that I'd have used it, but it was the end of a very long and busy season, I was overworked and overstressed, and I was still feeling the effects of that touch of the sun. Just to be sure, Peter Bosworth put his hand on the jack handle as well. I told Ralph that I was going to write out a cheque for him, giving him a partial refund, and would be putting him and his wife on a plane in Coen tomorrow, sending them both back south. I was thoroughly fed up with this bloke, never having struck anyone like it before. When I'd finished, Ralph stared at me for a moment or two and then said, "Well Goddamn, I back down." This took the wind out of my sails for a while, and always believing in human nature, I decided that I should give him another chance.

The next night we were on the Wenlock River, a spot where we were to split the party into two groups. The two Peters were taking their group in their two vehicles, up to the Cape, while I was taking the ornithologists in the party, into the Iron Range rain forest area, over on the East Coast. Neither Ralph nor his wife had any ornithological interests, so they were both in the Cape York party, a fact that pleased me no end.

Both parties returned five days later, right on schedule and I was keen to learn how Ralph had behaved while he was away. Apparently, he had been the perfect traveller, so I thought that he must have turned over a new leaf. This was not the case however, as no sooner had we travelled to where I was not able to fly him out, than he was up to his old tricks again. He was a lot more subtle this time, and in most instances, I was his prime target. If murder had been legal then he would be history, so I just had to tolerate him.

Finally, between Normanton and Cloncurry, things came to a head when we were at a little bush pub called Quamby. I owned the Birdsville pub at the time, and I was quite friendly with the publican at Quamby. We would at times, take over the kitchen and cook for the party, and on this occasion, we were having a few beers in the bar, and everyone was having a good time; even Ralph and his wife appeared to be enjoying themselves. I told the party that we would go down to the creek to set up our camp, and no sooner had I spoken than Ralph remarked, "another late camp." This was typical of his form since rejoining us at Wenlock River. We were serving the soup, (seem to have a lot of drama when we are serving the soup) with everyone sitting on stools around the campfire. I observed that Ralph wore a very smart, close fitting, mauve coloured shirt, with sleeves rolled up to the maximum, as well as mother of pearl buttons. After I had finished serving Ralph, I moved on to the next person, and I heard Ralph mutter in a low voice, just loud enough for me to hear, "We are gonna throw the book at this guy." Well! That was it; enough was too much. I dropped the soup pot and spun around, gripping Ralph by the front of his shirt, and pulling him up off his stool. As I did so there was a succession of ping, ping, ping sounds as several expensive mother of pearl buttons whizzed past my ear. I threw him back on his stool; (he didn't appear to have spilt any soup), turned around to the rest of the party, all transfixed with spoons full of soup, poised partway between bowl and mouth. (The floorshows were not usually this lively). I said to them "I wish to make an announcement." I then went on to tell them that, from that moment on, Ralph and his wife were to be confined to the 'fish tank'. This was that area of rear seating, in the older 'International' that Peter Coombe was driving. I told the pair that they could come out to sleep, and to go to the toilet, but that was it. You could have heard a shadow move until people went on eating, in stunned silence, with plenty of food for thought, that satisfied the appetite more than the soup.

The final six days were interesting, to say the least, in fact I had to pinch myself to remind myself at times, that this was really happening. Here were two clients, paying me to cart them around in a mobile prison. Mind you it was comfortable, the tucker was good, as was the scenery. This became the norm, and the rest of the party just accepted it. All along they had been very supportive, without being directly involved as, to a greater extent, were the two Peters. However, this was my problem and I would deal with it. Anyone who knows me will say how tolerant, patient, and even long suffering I usually am, but this situation was different. It was simply an indication of a couple of facts – how bad this bastard was, and that this year had been the busiest I had ever endured as a safari guide. This was the last trip of a frenetic season, and a culmination of these factors, produced this extraordinary situation. Anyway, that's the way I liked to see it, though others might say that I'd been in the bush for too long; I didn't think so. I've recently celebrated my sixty third birthday, and I feel that I still have a good few years left in the game yet.

As we headed south, a pattern was emerging. When we pulled up at little bush towns, the 'prisoners', as they were referred to, would spring out of the 'fish tank', and scuttle across to the pub. Soon after they would emerge, arms laden with six packs, head back for the 'Inter', and proceed to demolish the beer. It seemed that we almost needed another truck to cart the empties. I had to hand it to them; they could certainly hold their grog. At meal times someone would ask, "Have the prisoners been fed yet?" Someone would then take their meals over to them, not unlike a Macdonald's or a Hungry Jack's, though our tucker was better, and they didn't have a choice of menu. I couldn't help thinking that they were enjoying themselves, but I can't vouch for that.

When we eventually got back to Adelaide, we pulled up in North Terrace, opposite The Grosvenor hotel, and I expected trouble to erupt. People were saying their goodbyes, and as I approached Ralph and his wife, I was on the balls of my feet. To my amazement, he put out his hand, and as if nothing untoward had occurred, said to me, "Goodbye Rex, and thanks for a very enjoyable trip." As they walked off, shouldering numerous string bags full of bones, I remained rooted to the spot. It almost gave me an idea for another safari.

The Last Straw

4.

The Angry Imbiber

Since 1976, I had been operating one-day winery camel treks at McLaren Vale, as well as one-day treks through Hardy's scrub to the Onkaparinga Gorge. The routes taken are known intimately by me, as I frequented them regularly as a kid, growing up in McLaren Vale, particularly Hardy's scrub and the 'gorge'. My earliest memories are full of weekend and school holiday adventures to those areas, plus longer campouts in the adjacent Mount Lofty Ranges. I trapped many foxes, and I snared rabbits and hares, in and around Hardy's scrub, a square mile of bush between McLaren Flat and the Onkaparinga Gorge.

I loved that particular patch of bush, and a lot of my early birdwatching was carried out there, along with like-minded mates. I was the first one to alert various influential people in conservation circles, that the scrub was about to be cut up and sold. This eventually led to the Government's purchase of it, and its subsequent declaration as a conservation park. I was given official permission, by the then Director of National Parks and Wildlife, to continue operating my summer treks through the park, on a long established track. Eventually, a 'Friends of Hardy's Scrub' group was formed, a group that lobbied consistently to the current Director of NPWS, until my camels and I were banned from trekking in the park. Effectively, the best friend the scrub probably ever had, was denied access with his camels.

Now I'm a very reasonable person, and although I despise most forms of bureaucracy, I will go along with fair and sensible rulings. This situation, however, was so totally unfair, that I flatly refused to simply lie down on the matter, and buckle under the pressure of the lobby group. I decided then to do some lobbying of my own, setting out to prove beyond doubt, that the camel access did no damage, and in fact, contributed to the security and the welfare of the region; e.g. picking up rubbish, spotting for firebugs etc.

It took me a year, but I finally won that battle, though I didn't expect they would ever give up; there were some sensible, genuine people in that group, but unfortunately, they were in the minority. We used to have longer camps in the Onkaparinga Gorge area, shooting and birdwatching; in fact, I still have bird lists from that region, dating from the mid 1950s. On one birdwatching excursion, I was nearly drowned during a raft trip down a flooding river; four of us on two wooden doors, lashed together on six 4-gallon drums, forming a primitive raft. It was a wild, exhilarating ride, with not much serious birdwatching taking place, before we were suddenly jammed tight under a dead Red Gum tree, lying across the river. We had however, managed about ten miles of jet-propelled travel down the river.

I knew the wine country too, a lot of it being under Sheoak and Peppermint Gum, before the change to Grenache and Shiraz. My Dad, Max Ellis, grew up with most of the winemakers, so it was no trouble for me to be given private access, by all of the original (and some new) landowners. I could almost fill a small book with accounts of these summer day-trek operations, but will select just one interesting episode.

I had a large party of ten people, out one day on a winery trek, with ten camels and me to run the operation. At this stage, I was operating from some land that I still owned, adjacent to my old property, Douglas Scrub. Most parties are very well behaved, even though some become a little exuberant after a few wineries, but this mob was an exception; I really had my work cut out, keeping them in some semblance of order. I have since banned the practice, but this mob had the interesting habit of passing a bottle of port from camel to camel, as they travelled between wineries. We used to visit six different wineries, Amery, Seaview, Coriole, D'arenberg, Merrivale and Chalk Hill. One particular bloke, who stood about six feet tall and was a bit overweight, stood out from the others, and was my main concern. The temperature that day was around forty degrees, and the party was drinking plenty, such that, rather than a wine tasting exercise, this was taking on the appearance of a wine guzzling trek. Partway through the journey, the bloke in question had fallen off a few times, much to the delight of his companions, both male and female. Now I'm not too bothered about people falling off a hump, well into a winery trek, as they are normally quite relaxed and hardly seem to feel it.

After our visit to the final winery, Chalk Hill, we still had a bit over an hour's walk back to the camel depot, travelling through creeks, bush and vineyards, with a kilometre or so of road to finish off. No sooner had we got under way, than this bloke hit the deck again. It was like trying to carry a jellyfish, as I loaded him back onto his hump; he was fast approaching the paralytic stage. To make matters worse, none of his mates could care less about him, as they were also well under the weather. Ten minutes later, off he slipped again, sprawling in a Yakka bush. This effort of loading him back on board, on my own, was starting to wear me out, and I was fast becoming desperate. It went through my mind that I could perhaps emulate the western movie practice of hanging him over the saddle, with his wrists tied to his ankles, but I was afraid that he might crack his head on something. Soon after, as we headed through some half-cleared land, with many introduced olive trees, a dull thud signalled to me that I had one down again. This time I decided that enough was enough, and that dramatic problems demand dramatic actions. I grasped him by the ankles, and dragged him into the deep shade of a large olive tree, action that only invited a few giggles from the rest of the party. I then tied him by the ankles to two different trunks of the tree, some distance apart, and one wrist to another branch. This ensured his relative comfort, and enabled him to reach the water bottle that I had left for him. He was out to it.

I finished the trek, and then fronted the group, who were set to go home without him. (Who needs enemies with friends like that?) I approached the most sober looking member of the group, and made him accompany me back to the scene of the crime in my four-wheel drive, where things had changed dramatically. Our drunk was revved up like a turbo charged bull-ant who wanted to kill me. He might have had a go at it too, if I had untied him. Instead, I told him to grow up, and departed with my passenger, returning a while later with two vehicles, including his. I also had a bit of old rope with which I retied him, a difficult task, as the jellyfish had turned into a scorpion. I retrieved my valuable length of camel halter rope, and then departed, leaving his mate to sort him out.

As I drove home, the thought uppermost in my mind was, 'This bloke was actually paying me for this day out'. Takes all kinds.

5. Spuds and Water

In the early 1960s, I was spending part of the summer, working on the Nullarbor with a mate of mine called Len Johnson, who was a contract fencer. After I left the sheep station in 1966, I returned to the Nullarbor over a number of years, for a large part of several summers, it being off-season for the Safaris. In our team was Colin Bernhardt, a young bloke who owned his truck, and young Garry, Len's youngest son (12 years old). We were fencing about 40 miles south of the railway line on B.H. MacLachan's huge Rawlinna station, where I had previously been employed as a sub overseer.

Life had been pretty uneventful for the three weeks I had been there, until one day Len broke a part on his Atlas Copco jackhammer. They were noisy but necessary tools that we had to use for drilling through the very hard limestone. A hole had to be made for banging in the steel posts, and for the gelignite charge that we used, for blowing holes for strainer posts. Len decided that he would have to drive three hundred miles to Kalgoorlie for the jackhammer part. He decided that Colin, young Garry, and I should go off in Colin's Chevy truck, cutting posts for the 3-4 days he expected to be away.

Len headed off next morning, and we did likewise. The season had been good on the plain, and there was a sea of two-foot high speargrass, all the way to the horizon. We planned to drive west into the Myall Tree Belt on the edge of the plain, cut a load of the very hard Myall posts, and follow our tracks back to camp; Seemed like a good idea to all concerned. We headed off in good spirits, with Colin driving, me in the front with him, and Garry sitting on our swags on the back of the truck. We had a drum of water, one of fuel, and a bag of spuds, not a lot else because we were running low on stores, and Len was going to bring some back from Kalgoorlie.

The going was fairly slow, just poking along at around 15 miles per hour, mostly in second gear, and occasionally we would strike a big, open flat. There was plenty of topsoil here, without large limestone rocks, so we could fairly race along at around twenty-five miles per hour. We had been travelling for about three hours, when we suddenly staked a tyre, something that is always on the cards. We all hopped out and off to survey the damage. "Ah well", I said, "We'll have to put the spare on." I noticed Colin looking a bit embarrassed as he said, "Actually, I haven't got one with me." I thought this was a bit unusual and said "Well! Looks like we'll have to mend it." Colin looked even more embarrassed and said, "Er, I haven't got me jack with me." I took a little while to digest this information, then I suggested that we could stick a couple of blocks of wood, or a large rock, under the rear axle and dig out from under the wheel with a post hole shovel. I knew we had one of them, and every time you moved, you would trip over a large rock. By this time, Colin looked so miserable, that I started to feel sorry for him; he said that he didn't have his puncture gear (including a wheel brace) with him either. It appeared that some weeks ago, he had left his spare wheel, along with jack, wheel brace and puncture gear, in at Rawlinna. Never quite got to the bottom of why that was.

Well, the more we surveyed our situation, the more I started to wish I was somewhere else. To put it in a nutshell, we were 'snookered', 40 miles from our camp, too far to walk back on our tracks in the hot weather, and not much point anyway, we didn't have a radio transceiver, as no one worried about them in those days. We weren't going to starve or perish, we had a bag of spuds, forty gallons of water, tea, a little bit of flour, half a tin of jam, some sugar and one tin of fruit.

We were surrounded by a vast grassland, with only a couple of scraggy Myall trees, several hundred metres distant. We soon rigged a tarp off one side of the truck, and made ourselves relatively comfortable. That is where I spent three of the longest days that I can remember (or it would have been). The first afternoon was OK; we walked across and gathered firewood, which was in the Myall trees, but after that it was just a matter of sitting under the tarp and yarning. However, on the second day, that all changed, for me anyway. I was poking around under the seat of the truck, looking for something to read, apart from the jam tin label and the rego sticker, when I put my hand on something paper-like, and pulled out this old book. I quickly noted, with relief, that it wasn't a vehicle manual, but a book called *Moleskin Midas*, by Tom Ronan. I quickly got into it, and what a treasure trove it was. All about a weedy little bloke called Anthony Yeates, who was obsessed with owning his own station, set around the turn of the century at a fictitious location called Anderson's Yard, at about the position of the town of Camooweal, near the Territory/Queensland border. Tom Ronan was an Adelaide author who had been a station manager for many years, and wrote very entertainingly, with a lot experience. Most of the characters had nicknames, most often the case in the bush, and I could match up many of his characters with blokes I know.

One of the characters was called Two Mile Sheedy, a fencer who used to do two perfect miles of fence before his skin would start to crack, and then he would have to go away on a bender. When he returned, he would do two very doubtful miles of fence, before sorting himself out. Another immaculate two miles would follow, before the situation repeated itself. Although greatly exaggerated, it nevertheless did remind me of my mate, Len Johnson. The book was of small print, so it took me all of two days to read. During this time, my only complaint was the shocking tucker. We had boiled spuds three times a day, with no salt and with little else; It's a wonder I still eat them. Anyway, I was just finishing off the book, when we heard a vehicle coming. Colin and Garry seemed a lot more relieved than I did, when Len pulled up in his truck. I said, "How are you going Two Mile Sheedy?" and that name has stuck ever since, it was well worth my diet of spuds and water to discover *Moleskin Midas*.

6.

The Fencer & the Borer

Two old Nullarbor mates of mine, Len Johnson (alias 'Two-Mile Sheedy') and Peter Hogg, definitely have one thing in common. It has to do with their arrival at the developing Rawlinna Station, and it has to do with communication.

Rawlinna Station is a huge tract of country, (3,700 square miles) taken up by B.H. MacLachlan Pty Ltd in 1960. It was virgin country on the western edge of the Nullarbor, near the railway town of Rawlinna. Rod Campbell was the first manager, and I was there in the capacity of overseer in 1962, when these events occurred. Much of our work involved looking after the various requirements of the contractors, including borers, fencers and tank builders. One day Len Johnson (who later became 'Two-Mile Sheedy') and Jack ('Gelignite') Bailey arrived in at the station camp in an old Ford Thames truck.

There was a great urgency for a phone line to be built from the homestead (a 30' x 20' tin shed with dirt floor), to the township, a distance of seven miles. To contact the company headquarters in Adelaide, Rod had to drive into the township to use the phone, which wasn't very satisfactory.

So Len and Jack were straightaway sent to Goddard's Creek, one hundred and twenty miles east of the station camp, to cut a load of Gimlet posts for the phone poles. Goddard's Creek was located in the South Western part of the Great Victoria Desert, between Kalgoorlie and us. Gimlet is an extremely tough Eucalypt timber, once used in the Kalgoorlie mines, and very resistant to termites. Rod described the timber to the fencers, and off they went.

They arrived back a few days later, with a load of Salmon Gum, a far softer timber, unsuitable for the job. It was one of those very delicate situations; Rod couldn't accept it, getting Rod into trouble as well. Two-Mile Sheedy and Gelignite Jack (an ex SAS explosives expert) had driven far, and toiled hard in summer heat to cut the load. They simply had their timber mixed up, not being used to working in this part of the world. They were furious, and almost 'snatched their time' in the end. Rod put them on to some interior fencing, and Rod, Tilley (station hand) and I went to Goddard's and cut the Gimlet poles; we also erected the phone line.

Some time before Two-Mile Sheedy and Gellignite Jack's unfortunate phone pole exercise, Peter Hogg had a shorter but more dramatic 'communications' type experience. He'd had a long drive north from the Eyre Highway, across the plain to Rawlinna township with his boring rig, a lumbering ungainly vehicle. As he arrived in the town, he had a small mishap. Hopping out of the vehicle, he went into the tiny post office, run by a tall thin red headed chap - an officious man with a purple temper.

Peter asked, "What are those overhead wires out there mate?" "The main phone lines from east to west", replied the postmaster. "Well mate, I think we might have a little job to do, because I've just wiped half of them out with my derrick." The postie was furious, even when Peter pointed out that it really wasn't his business anyway. The upshot was that they both spent the afternoon up the rig, doing some temporary mends on the wires; caused quite a stir at the time.

Anyway, over the years, 'Two-Mile' and 'Hoggy' played an ongoing series of practical jokes against each other, with them occasionally getting out of hand. I will mention three such incidents.

The first concerned the Rawlinna Branch of the Royal Antediluvian Order of Buffaloes, the Buffalo Lodge, one of those mysterious men's secret societies, some would say. Peter was the Grand Wizard or whatever the boss is called, and 'Two-Mile' was a member. They met regularly in a small hall, the walls being constructed of railway sleepers, stacked one on top of the other. The members comprised mainly commonwealth railway workers, with some rabbit trappers and station blokes. Meetings began religiously at 8pm.

On this occasion, Two-Mile Sheedy had to drive his old Ford Thames in from his camp, forty miles south of Rawlinna. He arrived at about ten past eight, only to find that he had been locked out. Resplendent in his dark suit, (a strange sight in the Nullarbor) he knocked on the door, demanding to be let in. An officious railways petty official opened the small flap in the door, and told Two-Mile, in no uncertain terms, that he would have to wait until the business was concluded. A very unwise move, Two-Mile Sheedy didn't drive forty miles over some of the worst tracks in Australia, to be told he had to sit outside the hall for an hour. This was not a man to be reckoned with. Two-Mile is into direct action, and not one for the subtle approach. He climbed back into his truck put it into bottom gear, and crawled up to the side of the hall. When the bumper bar was against the railway sleeper wall, he revved up the motor and let out the clutch. The result was amazing, and is still discussed with awe to this day, the wall acted like a game of fiddlesticks, when the skewers are dropped on the table. Sleepers spun out everywhere, and luckily no one was hurt. Two-Mile's old truck, with headlights blazing like the eyes of an enraged bull, lurched several feet into the room and stalled.. Two-Mile Sheedy hopped out of the truck, and warned the railway clerk who had barred him earlier, 'to let him in the bloody front door next time'.

If this incident had taken place in a more civilized district, you could expect the repercussions to be severe and ongoing. But being Rawlinna, it's safe to say that for many of the assembled, it was a very welcome diversion, after all it wouldn't take much to repair the wrecked wall, a more difficult repair would be to the ego of the railway clerk. Also, Hoggy, while he gave the dramatic arrival of Two-Mile full marks for direct action, he was a bit upset about the subsequent shattering of decorum. He had recently been elevated to the position of Grand Wizard, and took the lodge seriously.

So it was that, while the meeting shelved the rest of the business, and got on with the 'harmony' (grog and songs basically), Hoggy went out to his truck and unloaded a five gallon drum of grease. He took it across to Two-Mile Sheedy's vehicle, which had been backed out and away from the hall, and while the 'harmony' (the official title in the Royal Antediluvian Order of Buffaloes, for the social part of their evenings) continued inside. Hoggy greased Two-Mile's truck. In fact, he put grease everywhere <u>except</u> in the grease nipples. Firstly, he put a 'gob' of grease on the driver's door handle, then he put a large amount on the running board, inside the cab. He put a small 'gob' on the ignition key, plastered it around the steering wheel and a goodly 'gob' on top of the gearstick. In addition, liberal amounts on the clutch, brake and accelerator pedals. Finally, he tipped the remainder of the drum (about 2 gallons) on the driver's seat.

Gingerly extricating himself from this 'grease trap', Hoggy took out Two-Mile's jack, and jacked up the rear driver's side wheel. He put a railway sleeper under that, jacked up the other wheel, and placed a railway sleeper under it as well. The scene was set, and Hoggy returned to the harmony.

Around one in the morning, Two-Mile, much the worse for wear, made his way with a drunk's concentration, toward his truck. Those who were sober enough, including the Grand Wizard, watched him. He stopped when he reached the driver's door, and went to take hold of the handle, his hand slipped off like he was grabbing a greased banana, and with repeated grabs he was unable to get a hold. Finally, when the bulk of the grease had been wiped off, he managed to open the door. The next phase was very dramatic. At the same time as he put his foot on the greased up running board, he grabbed the steering wheel to pull himself up into the cab. He appeared to do around three hundred and sixty degrees, landing flat on his back in the bulldust. This was appreciated hugely by the audience, and when the dust cleared, Sheedy made an interesting sight in his suit, sitting in the dust. He got to his feet, and with dogged determination, managed to scramble his way into the cab. He didn't appear to notice that he'd sat in the great gobs of grease on his seat.

Peering at the dashboard, he went for the starter key, only to have his thumb and index finger continuously slip off. By this time, the audience had all gathered closely around the truck, Two-Mile seemingly oblivious to them. He eventually latched on to the key and started the truck, but his foot slipped off the accelerator as he tried to rev the motor. Grabbing hold of the greasy wheel, he tried to depress the clutch, at the same time grabbing the gear stick. He didn't have much joy in either area, and at about this time, several of the wrapt audience slid to the ground in helpless mirth.

Finally, he managed to engage first gear, let out the clutch, and as far as he was concerned, headed off to his camp. The jacked up truck rear wheels were spinning, as Two-Mile shifted into second gear, which was as fast as he would normally drive over the limestone for the first ten kilometres or so. The next thing, he slumped forward on the wheel sound asleep; it had been a long hard night. The remaining onlookers headed off to their various abodes, leaving Two-Mile in a totally greased up situation. A rabbit trapper made the remark that, the "poor bastard probably won't go rusty for awhile"; someone turned the motor off.

Next morning, a few of the hardier revellers were out, sitting on the raised verandah with a 'hair of the dog', or a cuppa, all eyes riveted on Two-Mile, still in his truck. He was stuck fast in grease, and in exactly the same position as the night before.

Finally, he woke up, and true to form, not sporting a hangover. Those watching closely, said he closed his eyes for a bit, not believing quite what he saw. He reopened them for another go, and reality set in when he heard the laughter and comments. A couple of the blokes went over with a cold stubbie, and helped extricate him from the truck. A sight he was in his suit, with grease from toe to eyebrow, but Two-Mile was a professional, and took it well. He spent the morning cleaning up the truck, and himself, then drove out of town with a thoughtful look on his face. Mentally, he marked that one up to Hoggy.

The next shots in Two-Mile and Hoggy's private war were fired some months later, when I was working with Two-Mile Sheedy on a fence south of Rawlinna. It became very evident that there was an increasing smell of dirty socks in the camp, and one evening after work, I saw Two-Mile roll the socks off his feet, and practically stand them up against a Myall tree. I made reference to this, and he told me what he had in mind. I couldn't believe it! Well, then again knowing the history of these blokes, perhaps I could. Two-

Mile told me that he was going to have to wear the same socks for another three days (He had worn them for four days already), to make it a week. He had been running wire, which meant that we were walking for up to ten miles a day in hot weather. You can imagine what his socks were like, because he wasn't washing his feet for a week either. I was camped right over the other side of the camp, and south of him, so the evening 'doctor' didn't blow the smell toward me. The final few days, those socks fairly 'crackled' when he took them off; this man was totally dedicated.

When the week was up, we loaded our camp on the old Ford Thames, plus a 44' of water and one of petrol, and headed for Rawlinna. We were going to be away for a week, cutting posts in the Myall Belt, on the northwestern edge of the Nullarbor. We used mostly Myall fence posts, as it is one of the hardest timbers in the world. You rarely get a straight post, as they are a very gnarled tree, but the art of fencing with bush timber like this, is to line it up in the holes, so that your overall fence line appears straight. Far more interesting and satisfying than using treated pine posts. To get this load of posts, we would have to drive a round trip of some 300 miles.

We crossed the train line at Rawlinna Township, and headed the twenty miles north to Seemore Downs cattle station, where Hoggy had taken on the manager's job. Seemore Downs had been taken up by South Australian interests, some time before the current occupation of the western Nullarbor by pastoralists. It had a large unfinished stone homestead on it, but Peter and Margaret Hogg were living in an old railway sleeper hut. (Peter and Margaret purchased Seemore Downs some years later, and son Donald Hogg runs it at the present time). Two-Mile had done his homework well, he knew Peter and Margaret were away pulling a bore, and the station proved to be deserted as we pulled up in front of the hut.

As was the custom, we went inside and made ourselves at home. As I prepared a meal, Two-Mile Sheedy settled down to more serious business. He went out to the truck, took two shocking looking objects from out of the toolbox, along with a hacksaw blade and a thin round file. He bought them back inside, put a sock on the table, and started cutting it into rings with the hacksaw blade. When he had one and a half socks cut up, he reached up onto the mantle piece, and took down a huge shearers teapot. (Hoggy drank copious amounts of tea). Placing the teapot on the table, Two-Mile began stuffing pieces of his sock into the large spout, ramming them down with the round file. It was gross, but I looked on with fascination; a professional was at work here. When the one and a half socks had been rammed up (down?) the spout, Two-Mile went back out to the truck, and reappeared with a hand drill. He got me to hold the teapot firmly while he drilled a hole, around 5/16" in diameter, through the mass of petrified sock. He then dug out about half an inch of the sock from the end of the spout, so that it couldn't be seen by anyone inspecting the teapot. The whole project took about three quarters of an hour. Finally, he sat the teapot back on to the shelf. Next morning we headed off to cut our posts. We duly returned to our camp, without seeing Peter or Margaret, returning a different way through Naretha railway siding.

A week or two went by as we continued fencing. We were getting low on fuel and stores, so planned a trip to the railway store at Rawlinna. By the time we drove the slow 70 Kilometres there and back, plus time there, it was a day lost, so we sort of looked at those trips as a day off. At that time, Margaret was working part time at the post office, and I called in for a yarn. I asked the usual "how's things?" and with a gleam in her eye, she recounted a little drama.

Peter was a great tea drinker, consuming numerous pannikins each day. On returning to the homestead after pulling the bore, he resumed drinking the tea from the big teapot. After several brews, he asked Margaret if she had changed the brand of tea, and when she said no, he muttered, "well it doesn't taste the bloody same." Over the next few days, he complained regularly about it, and a few mornings later, Margaret was shaking the tea leaves out of the pot outside, when an object dropped to the ground. Curious, Margaret picked it up, wiping the tealeaves off it. She could see that it was a shred of cloth, and it had writing on it. Straightening it out, she was interested to observe the word, Johnston. It was a nametag off one of Two-Mile's sox. Margaret knew of Joyce's habit of putting nametags on all of Len's clothes, and the whole tea drama suddenly became clear. I filled her in on the whole story and we had a good laugh.

Peter found out about it, and was furious, vowing vengeance. A couple of other incidents occurred that I wasn't involved with, but I was around when the straw that broke to camel's back occurred.

It happened one hot weekend in February, when a few of us were in town (Rawlinna). Peter was boring for water north of the town, and was carting water from Rawlinna. The town supply was carted by rail from Port Augusta in water 'Gins' - large railway trucks converted to tankers. These were pumped into a large concrete tank that was used by the old steam trains.

Peter would drive into town in his ancient dilapidated K-9 International truck, devoid of doors and other 'unessentials'. On this occasion, he pulled up next to the railway tanks and began siphoning water into his 400 gallon tank on the back of his truck. It was a slow process, and while it filled, he went over to the Ganger's place to have a cup of tea or two. Sheedy was in town also, sitting on another railway worker's verandah, observing Peter's activities with interest. As soon as Peter disappeared into the Ganger's house, Two-Mile sprang into action. He got hold of a railway oxy set (oxyacetylene cutting set), and keeping the truck between himself and the Ganger's house, he set about his work. What he did, was to cut halfway through both sides of the rear chassis of the truck, and then extricated himself, struggling back to the shed, dragging the oxy cylinders like an ant with a large crumb. In less than half an hour, he was back on the same verandah, about to witness a 'desert drama'.

Hoggy duly appeared on the Ganger's verandah, and walked across the rocky, pot-holed stretch of ground that served as Rawlinna's main street. The word had spread like wildfire through the single line of houses, and every verandah was a balcony at the theatre. Hoggy switched the water off, hopped into the K-9, and slowly headed toward the edge of town, bouncing over the rough ground. The eager onlookers were suddenly rewarded for their vigilance. There was a grinding crunch, and the K-9 stopped, and seemed to hunch its back as the chassis broke. It was probably as close as anyone ever came to drowning on the Nullarbor.

A huge geyser of water shot off the top of the tank, completely drenching Hoggy in the doorless cab. It very quickly drowned the opened engine (no bonnet either). The whole line of houses erupted in laughter, as something looking like a drowned rat slid out of the cab. It was too much for Hoggy, he strode across the flat, heading in Two-Mile's direction, and one of their rare periodic blues began.

They were never very long-lived, and this one was no exception. The pattern was always the same. Hoggy would go after Two-Mile, swinging huge 'haymakers', while Two-Mile would jab him on the nose with straight lefts, usually connecting, and these only succeeded in infuriating Peter all the more. Eventually one of his haymakers would connect with Two-Mile's head, and that was the end of the fight. As always, he would pick Two-Mile up, and wiping his own bloody nose, they would head for the nearest house for a cup of tea or two, and so the game went on.

Author's note:

Peter Hogg (born in Kinclaven, Scotland) actually died in Kalgoorlie, playing his beloved bag pipes. Although, he probably would have given himself another twenty years or so (he was in his fifties when he died). He would agree that he couldn't orchestrate his demise any better, even if he had tried.

7.

Sir William and Buy More Wool

It was 1964 and the wool industry was going through one of its periodical troughs. The high profile Sir William Gunn was often in the news, trying to get the industry back on its feet. At the time, I was overseer on Bimbowrie station, a 300 square mile sheep run to the north of Olary, and around 150 kilometres west of Broken Hill.

We were boiling the billy, one day in December, after five of us had been mustering on horses, and we were enjoying our camp lunch in the welcome shade of a gum tree. Topics around the campfire are many and varied, and eventually the conversation got around to the state of the wool industry. One of the station hands sort of terminated the discussion, asserting "Well there's nothing us blokes can bloody well do about it."

Later that afternoon, I was sitting on my horse behind a small mob of sheep, still thinking about our lunchtime conversation, when slowly a bit of an idea took place in my head; why not capture a large billy goat, christen it Sir William, and take it for a trip to Adelaide? We could put a sign on it saying, "Sir William - Buy More Wool" and let it go at some crowded destination. With a bit of luck it should attract some publicity, and that could be our modest effort to strike a blow as it were, for our embattled industry. By the time I had ridden to the station, I had convinced my kelpie that it was a good idea, and after the evening meal, I floated the idea to the boys. They agreed that it was a good idea, so long as I was the one that did the letting go of the goat.

Christmas was only a week away, and I had arranged to meet mates of mine in Adelaide, the Campbell brothers from Kybo Station. So it was that two of the blokes, Jack and Stanley, accompanied me to a dam at the back end of the run. It was Saturday afternoon, and there were plenty of wild goats running out there, so I was pretty confident of getting my goat. Feral goats are, of course, a menace to the environment, particularly in the arid zone, where they do almost as much damage to mature vegetation as rabbits.

The policy of the Bimbowrie Station owner was to encourage the staff to muster goats, and to sell them to the Peterborough meat works. We were allowed to pocket the proceeds, which was quite a bonus for us, as mature goats were bringing around ten dollars per head at the time. It was exciting, and often dangerous work, as much of the of the mustering was carried out in rough range country; the Billys in particular would always break away from the mob, so we would have to gallop after them among the rocks, to turn them back in. However, we enjoyed the work, and the extra money, and we felt that we were doing our bit for the environment as well.

We parked the Scout in the scrub near the dam, and made ourselves comfortable. After an hour or so, a mob of around twenty goats came in to water. The main reason for waiting near the dam was that goats are a lot easier to run down with a belly full of water. We noticed that there was a large white billy, with a very wide set of horns, and as soon as I spotted him, I thought, 'that will be Sir William'. After the mob had watered and had moved out from the dam, I sent Tibun, my black kelpie, around the back of the mob. She went around them like a black streak, and at the same time, the three of us blokes ran toward the milling mob, some 200 metres away. As we approached the mob, 'Sir William' broke away, in true billy goat style, heading for some distant hills. The three of us took after him, with Tibun bouncing around in front of the goat, grabbing his beard, getting shaken off, and not having any effect in pulling him up.

After a while, Jock dropped out of the race, while Stanley, Tibun and I kept on, not narrowing the twenty metre gap at all. I thought that this would be my only chance to get my goat, before I left for Christmas. Gradually we narrowed the gap, and just when I thought I couldn't go another step, Tibun managed to slow him for a couple of valuable seconds. Stanley and I fell upon him, hanging on to him like grim death. We lay there for a while, just until we could summon enough energy to get up. Not having any rope, I took my belt off, and tied up three of Sir William's legs. We left him there under a tree, while we walked a good kilometre back to the vehicle, and to where we'd left Jock.

Picking up our cargo, we headed back to the station, where I tied Sir William to a star post, out the back of the men's quarters. Two days later, we loaded a still very feral billy into the boot of my Peugeot car, and I headed south for Christmas. After around thirty kilometres, I arrived at the little outback town of Olary, our nearest settlement. I pulled up at the store, and as Mrs. Frost was putting some fuel in the tank, a very strange bellowing type noise, came from within the vehicle. Mrs. Frost asked me what it was, and I said, "It's just the air conditioner."

That evening, I arrived at McLaren Vale, where my parents lived, and talked my folks into letting me tie up Sir William in the back yard. I nearly lost him during his unloading, because he was fairly stirred up. There may well be the odd reader that considers this little exercise a bit cruel; well let's put it this way, if Sir William had stayed back at Bimbowrie, his fate would have been to be shot or mustered, and sent to the Peterborough meatworks. This way he was probably going to end up as someone's lawnmower.

Having made Sir William comfortable, but not necessarily welcome in my folks' backyard, I arranged to meet the Campbell boys. Their father was the caretaker of Edments building in Rundle Street, and his residence occupied much of the top floor of the building, a spot where Rod and Graeme stayed on their infrequent trips to Adelaide. The boys were to drive to McLaren Vale on Boxing Day, to pick up Sir William and me.

After a pleasant family Christmas, in which Sir William enjoyed a number of exotic tastes, Rod arrived in his Toyota Stout ute. We tied Sir William's legs again, placed him in the ute, and threw a tarp over him.

Being the day after Christmas, the traffic situation on that late afternoon was pretty grim. While we were held at the traffic lights at Reynella, we noticed that a traffic cop on a bike, had pulled up on our right, next to Rod. A few seconds later, Sir William gave his usual bellow from under the tarp, and the next ten seconds or so seemed to take an eternity to pass, particularly for Rod. The traffic cop fixed him with a penetrating stare, and we reckoned that he thought Rod was having a go at him, you know, taking the Mickey out. The seconds ticked by, the lights remained on red, and still the cop glared at Rod, from a distance of about six feet. Finally, the lights turned green, so Rod dropped the clutch with a degree of relief. We duly arrived in the city, and parked the ute in a side street, next to Edments building. Graeme joined us then, so we went off for a couple of beers and a feed.

When we returned, at about 6pm, there was a small crowd gathered around the ute, so we decided to stop and assess the situation.

Over our meal, we had fixed on a plan to give Sir William maximum exposure. It was our intention to phone the *Advertiser* to say that a happening was to take place in Hindley Street, at a quarter to eight that evening. We had a sign prepared 'Sir William - buy more wool', to tie across the billy's wide horns. We planned to release him from an alley, near the Wests picture theatre, where we reckoned he would burst upon the scene at one of the most crowded times. Traffic was reduced to a crawl, so no damage would be done, and in any case, it was for the sake of the wool industry, wasn't it?

But now we could see that our plan was at risk, and as we approached the edge of the group, we soon found out what the attraction was. Every couple of minutes or so, Sir William would give his strange bellow, and rear up under the tarpaulin. If you didn't know what was under there, it was a better crowd stopper than the best of the buskers. I suggested to Rod and Graeme that we ought to cut our losses and take the hat around.

If we were to let him go as planned, someone probably had our rego number and could dob us in, which would be embarrassing all round. The next thing that happened, exacerbated our situation even further. Rod and Graeme's sister, Janet (a mischievous wench) suddenly hung her head out of the sixth floor window and hollered, "You blokes can't leave your ute there, you'll get a ticket!" We hastily evaporated into the building to regroup.

What a stuff up, and what to do with Sir William. Graeme suddenly had an idea that seemed like the best compromise around; we would offer Sir William to the zoo for lion meat. This seemed like the best way out for us, so we rang the zoo to see if we could unload Sir William; but no one answered.

After waiting til the crowd dispersed somewhat, we hopped in the ute, and drove down Frome road to the edge of the Zoological Gardens. Here we found a doubtful piece of rope, lifted out the cargo, and hastily tied him to a tree near the wall of the zoo. It was our intention to return in the morning, and offer

The Drunk's Close Shave

Sir William to the zoo, although I was starting to feel a bit low about it. Sir William and I went back a fair way, and he was starting to grow on me. By this time it was dark, and we had just got back into the ute, when Sir William was suddenly free. We are not sure if he just broke the rope, chewed it through, or what. Like a white ghost, he was streaking across the parklands, heading for the rear of the Adelaide Hospital.

It was then that we saw a drunk carrying a bottle (presumably) in a paper bag, directly in the path of our escapee. The distance was about one hundred and fifty metres, and it seemed to us that the inebriated one was going to be flattened. However, Sir William passed, about a metre or two in front of the drunk, who dropped his paper bag and struck a stance of amazement. He remained frozen in this position, as Sir William disappeared into the gloom of the hospital area, while we headed off for another much needed beer.

Next morning we listened to all the news bulletins, and read the *Advertiser* from front to back, but nary a mention of Sir William. I guess we'll never know, but you can bet your life he ended his days as somebody's suburban lawnmower, with a story to tell.

8. You're on the List

In 1960, I was working as a jackeroo on Lilydale Station, in the north east of South Australia. In those days, stations still carried plenty of men, and as well as five of us jackeroos, there were half a dozen station hands on the property.

In the main, the station-hands were experienced men, often having spent many years on stations throughout the country. Some of them didn't have a lot of time for us jackeroos, who were young blokes, not long out of school. We were virtually apprentices, learning the sheep station business, and hoping later to become overseers and managers. However, by and large, we co-existed pretty well, with a fair bit of, mostly good natured rivalry amongst us.

Among the station hands was a man called Ken, and from the very first day Ken had arrived on the station, he maintained that he was a communist. Of average height and build, he had a very morose nature, and we all presumed that he spent a lot of time brooding about the supposed injustices of the capitalist system. He seemed to be totally preoccupied with the situation, whether it was because he wasn't the most scintillating of company, or whether most of the blokes were a bit wary of him; they generally gave him a wide berth. I hadn't taken a lot of notice of him, until one day, Ivan the manager, sent me out to pull down an old fence, and accompanying me were two station hands, Bill and 'Ken the Commo'.

Now the curious thing about this jackeroo - station hand thing, where it applied to the Mutooroo Pastoral Co, was this. On a job such as this, the jackeroo was put in charge, of course, which was supposed to give us experience in handling men; in most cases, it wasn't too successful. In this case, they had an 18-year-old first year jackeroo in charge of two very experienced station hands. The result, most of the time, was that the station hands called the tune, and lumped the responsibility on the jackeroo if the job went wrong; and pity help any jackeroo that had delusions of grandeur, and started pulling rank on the station hands!

Anyway, on this occasion, it was my first job where I was officially in charge. I was pretty nervous, but things started off OK, because they let me drive the tractor while they sat on the back of the four wheel trailer, (we didn't have far to go). My authority stopped as soon as we reached the job site. The blokes just began pulling this old fence down, as though I wasn't there. In analysing this, I thought. 'Fair enough, I suppose, the job is straight-forward, enough, and doesn't need any direction from me'. I did feel a bit superfluous though. It was a very hot February day, and we all worked in silence until lunchtime. A fire was lit, the billy was boiled, and we all sat under the trailer, because there was no shade on the claypan.

Bill lapsed into his midday snooze, but Ken gave me a first hand account of his views on society in general. There was a pause after ten minutes, and then he said, "I've got a list you know." I took another bite of my peanut paste and Prince Engelbert plum jam sandwich, and then started to listen with interest, tempered with a small amount of trepidation. He went on to tell me how the general manager of the Mutooroo Pastoral Co was at the top of his list, then the Lilydale manager, Ivan, followed by Andy the overseer. He also mentioned another couple of names from other stations where he had worked.

After a while, Ken went silent, the only sound being that of a crow on a dead mulga, half a kilometre away, and Bill's light snoring. I had heard of the reason that Ken had this list, but I was curious to hear Ken say it himself. I was also a bit scared, but taking another mouthful of tea, I asked him why he had the list. Ken looked me straight in the eye and said "That's my hit list, I'm gunna shoot the bastards." Hastily returning to my peanut paste and jam sandwich, I felt thankful that I hadn't started giving out orders left, right and centre, as soon as we arrived on the job. The rest of the day passed without incident, but it wasn't without quite a bit of food for thought.

A couple of months later, Ivan told me to take the truck, along with Bill and Ken, and go out to Diamond Dam yards to pick up four rams. Seemed like a simple enough job, so I went and found Bill and Ken, lurking in the blacksmith's, and being very careful not to give them a direct order, made it known to them that it wouldn't be a bad idea if the three of us took a drive out to Diamond Dam yards to pick up four rams.

While we are on this subject, let's just dwell on it for a minute. You will notice that, in the outback, many (most) successful bosses will not give a direct staccato type order to their men; It's the old Australian thing about men being, supposedly, equal. So a good boss will usually 'boundary ride' the subject a bit, sort of suggesting, rather that telling men to do something. You will see this, to some extent, in the cities as well, but it almost becomes an art in the backcountry.

Anyway, getting back to it, we drove the truck the five miles out to Diamond Dam, backed up to the yards, and surveyed our load, four big shorn rams, in a yard about an acre in area. The way the men were muttering, I got the feeling that this wasn't going to be a piece of cake. We didn't have a dog between us, so we had to run them down, and after about ten minutes, we had one in the back of the truck, a six ton Bedford with a stock crate. We were already buggered because it was hot, though Ken wasn't too bad, but Bill looked like he was about to pop a blood vessel, not being the fittest man on the run.

The next two that we loaded took half an hour, and we were all in various stages of being ragged around the edges. After a brief spell and a suck on the water bag, the three of us converged on the big Bungaree bred merino ram, standing and stamping his front foot on the ground. We rushed him in unison, and the ram did a half circle, heading for the fence. Before we could catch him, he hurdled the fence like an overweight antelope, and headed through the bluebush for the Blackoak scrub in the distance. Bill yelled, "get the *!+!!**/*! Mongrel", and we all set off to try to catch him. Almost immediately, Bill dropped back and stopped, leaving Ken and me to soldier on. Some of you will know what it's like; Ken and I were running side by side, the ram just six feet in front of us. Like marathon runners, after twenty miles, there was no way that any more speed could be squeezed out of us. However, we were determined to get our ram, but by employing different methods. So it was that, at the same time, Ken threw the last of his dying energy into a flying rugby tackle, while I took a mighty jump, hoping to grab the ram by the rump. What entailed turned out good, but only for the ram. As Ken hit the ground, my right boot landed fair and square on his neck, grinding his head into the dirt. I fell over, while the ram kept on, cantering at that maddening slow place, eventually to disappear into the distance. Ken ignored my profuse apology at he rose unsteadily to his feet, his head angled to one side. We walked back to where we'd left Bill and the truck, and drove back to the station in stony silence, to where I had to report on a job that was only three quarters successful.

Next morning, when I was servicing the truck, I saw Bill walking across the yard toward me, obviously on a mission. He told me that Ken had a message for me. "He said to tell you that you're on the list!"

9.

An African Experience

GETTING THERE – THE U.K.

In 1973, Patti and I had one of our best years in the safari business. We were married in 1971, and at this stage, had not started a family, so we decided that we would head overseas. I had always had a great desire to get to Africa, and at that time, the cheapest way was to spend forty-two days in Europe en route. That seemed like a good idea, so we decided to do it.

I had written a good number of letters to offbeat, African Safari operators, trying to find the right sort of operation. I had this idea of setting up a reciprocal, client swapping arrangement with an operator over there, which meant that our expenses could be claimed as a tax deduction. I eventually found my man, and arranged to visit him in late January 1974.

We duly arrived at Heathrow airport, London, on a wet night in December, and booked into a pub. My previous overseas experience had been a three-week trip to Fiji, (I had gone there to talk a mate out of marrying a Fijian girl and almost didn't return myself), but this was Patti's first trip away from good old Oz. After a couple of days in London, seeing the sights and marvelling at the Crown Jewels in the Tower of London, we took a train down to a town called Totnes in Devon, which just happened to be the area that my Dad's side of the family had come from, four generations earlier. I had a mate living there at the time, who was a native of the area, and we were going to stay with him for three weeks or so.

I intended to do a few slide shows on Outback Australia, as William John Wills of Burke and Wills fame, hailed from Totnes, so there was perhaps, more than the usual interest in Australia. This, we hoped, would pay for our board and lodgings. I had also been lined up for some part time work with a contractor, cutting down Dutch Elm trees. The tragic Dutch Elm tree disease was rampant at the time and these lovely trees were being cut down, over the length and breadth of the country. My job was to cut up with an axe, firewood size pieces, from limbs that had been cut down by the contractor with a chain saw. Anyway, we settled into our upstairs lodgings, very cosy, with the seemingly constant rain falling outside.

I've always subscribed to the theory that, when in Rome, one should do what the Romans do, so I got hold of a checkered peaked cap, some old working clothes, and a sugar bag to carry my lunch in. Each morning, I would set out on the couple of kilometres to work on the hills, overlooking the town where Elm trees were being cut. On the way, I had to pass through a walkway at the back of a line of terrace houses. Local tin miners resided here, and at precisely ten to eight every morning, around a dozen doors would open simultaneously, and from each of these doorways, a man in a peaked cap and bag over his shoulder, would step out, turn right and head off into the bleak weather. I would be going against the grain, as it was, in the opposite direction.

On the first morning I was totally ignored, but I didn't say anything either. However, on the second day, I picked out a bloke, and as I passed him I said "how are y' going mate, awright?" Well, it was as if I'd hit him on the head with my sugar bag. He stopped, and I could feel him looking after me as I continued on my way. Next morning, he was ready for me, asking me more or less, what I was up to etc. etc. This resulted in a nice little two-minute yarn each morning for the next week, while my work was in the area. It was just one of those little experiences that you remember.

I would spend the morning cutting up Elm trees in the fog and drizzle, a bright spot being when Patti arrived mid morning with my lunch, and to spend an hour or so stacking timber. The real bright spot of this operation was one day, when the sun actually appeared for five minutes and Totnes was revealed below in all its glory, with the ruined castle in the centre of the town taking pride of place.

One night I went to a wine and cheese tasting party, and met one of Britain's leading adventure novelists, the late Desmond Bagley. When he learnt of my occupation in Australia, he became very excited. Apparently, his chief competition, Hammond Innes, had recently released a best selling novel called *The Golden Soak*, set in Australia. As Australia was one of the few major countries where Bagley had not set a book, he was keen to do so, wanting to discuss with me the possibility of a future contract. He had a very severe stutter, but I noticed that, as his Scotch consumption increased, his stutter practically disappeared. We arranged to meet the following afternoon, after my woodcutting job, and duly did so at one of the High Street pubs,

After a few pots of warm English beer, Desmond invited me back to his very large house, where he was batching with his poodle; his wife was absent in France. He took me into a very large room, remarkable for two features.

The walls were completely taken up with glass case shelving, one half consisting of books, and the other of grog; an amazing collection of both. He asked what seemed a bit of a trick question. "Would you like a drink?" "Yes, I wouldn't mind." I replied. "What sort of drink would you like?" he asked. "I'd like a beer." I replied. "What sort of beer?" asked Desmond. I thought for a moment, managing to recall a fairly obscure brand of German beer which I named. He replied, "Easily fixed", returning shortly with a bottle of the said beer; I was impressed. To cut a long story short, we soon switched to Scotches, talking through the afternoon, as the rain continued outside. My recollection of anything after the second or third scotch is almost non-existent. I consider myself to be a fair drinker, but this was one hell of a session, plus I am not really a spirits drinker.

My next recollection was that of standing on his porch with a raised umbrella in my hand, launching myself into the rain, with no real idea of my directions. At one stage, I recall a little old lady bailing me up. I must have mumbled a request for information, because she set me off on another course. This was only about the second time in my life that I have been drunk enough to cause me, to all intents and purposes, to be out of control. I could walk OK, and I had in my mind a destination, but that was about it. After some time, more by good luck than good management, I found myself at the top end of High Street, and eventually to my quarters.

Patti was not impressed, knowing that I had a slide show and talk to attend, in a couple of hours time. She bullied me into a bath of cold water, which had the effect of giving me a clearer perspective on the proceedings, although still in no state to present a slide/talk. My memories of the evening are hazy at best, but from various reports, I must have got through the evening OK.

After travelling to Scotland, we were ready for a short stint in Europe, before heading to Africa. A few days before we were due to travel to Spain for a week, we rang an Italian couple, the Grassis, to say "gooday." They had joined us on a vehicle crossing of the Simpson Desert the previous year, and we had got on very well together, even though Enzo couldn't speak a word of English, and Nella could speak only English, but not 'Australian'; they were in their seventies. Nella answered the phone, and straight away invited us to come and stay with them at their summer residence at Bordighera, on the Italian Riviera. I said that we would love to, but wouldn't have the time after spending a week in Spain. After discussing that, she exclaimed, "you must not go to Spain — it is full of barbarians — you must come straight to us." Well, who were we to argue? Spain would just have to wait, so I instantly agreed and arranged to meet them in Nice.

Getting There – Europe

We duly arrived at Bologne in France, after travelling across the English Channel in the hovercraft. We were to spend a night in Paris, and wanted to stay overnight in a typical small French hotel. Eventually, after travelling from Bologne to Paris, we made a booking at one that was located in a side street off the Champs d'elysees. The Peugeot cab (always happy to ride in a Peugeot, because I am something of a Peugeot aficionado) dropped us off at the pub, and it looked like what we were after. Behind the reception was a small elderly French woman, dressed in black, who didn't look too friendly. We booked in, and when I asked about an early breakfast, she informed me that they didn't serve breakfast. I knew that the French weren't big on breakfast, but I had to try. I then suggested that we could go into the kitchen and knock ourselves up a toasted sandwich in the morning. Well, that made her incredible in stature. She flew off the stool and, I suspect, told us off in French. We fled in dismay, annoyed because our payment was supposed to cover breakfast.

After an interesting night, working out bidets and things, we descended the spiral staircase just after daylight next morning. It was as cold as buggery, and I was hungry as hell, and couldn't help but notice the delicious aroma of cooked bread as we approached the bottom floor. I thought "Mine Host has decided to knock us up some breakfast after all." On approaching the reception desk, we were confronted with a huge bunch of metre-long bread rolls, wrapped in paper, with the ends protruding. I said to Patti, "We'll have a couple of them." Now she is more law abiding than I am, and I think she was suggesting that my idea was, well, thieving. But I disagreed, saying that we had already paid for breakfast. I looked upon this as poetic justice, though a thermos of coffee wouldn't have gone amiss! Anyway, I grabbed one, and stuck it down the front of my overcoat, with the top sticking out, as out of the door we went, me chewing on the delicious roll, pushing it up from well down past my navel, as I worked away on the top.

Patti kept looking over her shoulder, expecting to see a flock of gendarmes running us down, but at this hour, the street was deserted. We caught a train, after a coffee at the railway station. A pleasant day was had on a very comfortable train, travelling across France. The picture-book countryside was very easy on the eye, and in what seemed like no time, we were pulling into Nice railway station.

It occurred to us that we might have a bit of trouble finding the Grassis in the large crowd, but we walked into the building. There was a loud "Rex!" and I saw the head and shoulders of Enzo above the crowd. He gave Patti and me a huge bear hug in the European manner, and he and Nella led us out of the railway station, to where an immaculate black Lancia was parked. After a drive of less than and hour, we arrived at their summer villa, cut into a cliff, with dramatic views of Bordighera and the Mediterranean. Our next week was very memorable, bordering on luxury, with some very different experiences for Patti and me.

There were five resident servants, and the service began with an early morning cuppa in bed. From there, we would gravitate to the patio for breakfast, where breathtaking views took in the Italian Riviera. Over to one side was Monaco, and on a clear day, you could probably see Princess Grace hanging out her washing. The week passed quickly, and most days, Enzo and Nella drove us to places like Monte Carlo Casino, up into the hills where we had coffee in little villages, watching old men play their Bocce bowls.

There were hair-raising shopping trips with Nella in her tiny Fiat. We would roar down off the mountains, with her hand constantly on the horn, and Patti and I thinking our numbers were definitely up, but we survived. Then, on the weekend, we put on the best we had and went promenading, a very Italian thing to do. We would all link arms, and then with hundreds of others, march up and down the Esplanade; all checking out what each other was wearing; pretty amusing.

Breakfast on the Run

Then there was our final night, a Saturday, when we were to go to another of their friends' places, a large house in the town of San Remo. This was a formal dinner party where they were to show the film that Nella shot of their Simpson Desert crossing. It was a very detailed account of the trip with not much unrecorded. Nella said they would sit us next to a doctor who spoke English, but after an initial greeting, he ignored us for the rest of the evening.

So, Patti and I gradually worked away at the excellent Italian red wine, slowly sinking into the excellent Italian furniture. Next thing, I was aware that a screen was up, and the film was being shown. I was taking it all in, when I saw our vehicles pull up on the banks of the flooding Eyre Creek, There I was pulling out the shot gun, and shooting a couple of wood ducks. What sobered me up was seeing myself strip off all of my clothes, (I had thought I was on my own.) and wading out into the river and swimming for the ducks. I collected the ducks and swam back to the shallower water, where I began wading into shore, with my Family Jewels very much exposed. I had suddenly become aware of Nella filming, and could be seen to hastily hang the ducks in a strategic position. I noticed the laughter in the room building up, and when I moved the ducks, the room broke out into clapping and cheering. I have to say that I was pretty embarrassed, but who was I to spoil their fun. It was a good grand finale to a very entertaining week.

Finally to Africa - Kenya

A few days later, we flew from Athens, across the Sahara, bound for Nairobi. In Kenya, we had a transit stop at Entebbe airport in Uganda. It was now January and the tropical heat was a welcome change from the European winter. Idi Amin was in power, but he wasn't yet infamous for his atrocities, and Entebbe airport hadn't yet been shot up by the Israelis, in the famous hostage rescue. As we walked into the airport terminal, we couldn't help but notice the huge sign that said "Forbidden - do not photograph the Ugandan Airforce." Scattered around were a couple of tired Mustangs, and a DC3 with one wing drooping. I was tempted, but thought better of it.

We reboarded and headed for Kenya, and there was one amusing incident on that flight. Someone had ordered a bottle of red wine, up the front of the aircraft, and in due course, the African steward went to pick up the empty bottle. As he did so, he walked back down past our seat, and something made me turn around to watch him. I witnessed something you probably wouldn't ever see on a Qantas flight. There was obviously some wine left in the bottle, and as he walked the last thirty feet or so of the aisle, the steward raised the bottle to his mouth and drained it. I remarked to Patti, that they sometimes do things a bit differently over here.

After landing at Nairobi, we found a cab and headed for a hotel. We were in the process of booking in, when a Land Rover pulled up out the front, and a dark haired lady in her fifties came flying through the doors. It was Jean Seed, wife of Freddie Seed, the owners of Samburuland Safaris. These were the people that I had arranged to do a safari with. Jean told us that we didn't want to book into the pub, that she had accommodation for us at her place, on the outskirts of Nairobi. So, we piled our luggage into the Land Rover and headed out there. Freddie ran part hunting, part photographic safaris, but he was away on Safari, so we were unfortunately not going to be able to see him. The house was full of kids, home from boarding school, so we were settled in a large tent on the back lawn, but for a tent, it had a few mod cons.

Freddie had arranged for his partner, Len Bonnett, to take us on a three-day safari to Northern Kenya. The main idea was to search for what was reputedly the world's largest elephant named Ahmed, who was most often seen near Marsabit in the north. The following day was spent relaxing, while Len finished preparations for the safari. We were to travel in a dark green Land Rover, with a roof hatch, that allowed for standing on the rear seat, sticking your head out above the roof for filming and observing. The last thing loaded was a little Negro bloke, who was wedged into a rear corner like an old boot. He seemed very pleased to be aboard, however.

We headed off on a highway to the north, travelling for three hours, before turning off into one of Freddie's hunting blocks, leases set aside mostly for hunting activities, and we had the area to ourselves. There were numerous antelope, some zebras and a couple of giraffe, which was very exciting for Patti and me. Len selected a campsite, and we started to get set up. Jundy, the Negro bloke, was like a blur, as he started putting up the tents. I went to help him, but Len quickly called me away to have a pink gin. I didn't feel too happy about that, but Len explained that it was a matter of pride for Jundy to set up the camp, that was his job, and there was probably a thousand others lined up for it, back in Nairobi. Old habits die hard but, after a couple of pink gins, I thought it would be within the realms of possibility to get used to the situation. When in Rome etc.

We took a walk while Jundy was preparing our meal. Len carried a rifle, but wasn't expecting any problems. There were numerous Dik Dik, a small hare-like antelope, Thomson's gazelle and zebras in the distance. Of particular interest were the Gwyder birds, with their long tails, hanging down like lengths of flypaper, and the stately secretary birds, a crane-like bird with a large crest that stalked around in a very officious manner.

Jundy was a good cook, and we had braised meat and a vegetable pie, with tinned fruit and jelly for desert. I asked Len if it would be possible to camp outside the tent, but he told me that he had a German client who did that, a year or two ago. A hyena bit his face off. I got rid of that idea very smartly. The night noises contrasted well with the Australian bush. There were lions roaring, not too far away, the weird cackle of hyenas, plus numerous others that I couldn't identify.

Next morning, after a brisk walk, we spent most of the day in the hunting block. After lunch, with good game viewing near a water hole, we came across a herd of elephants, half a dozen or so, accompanied by a big bull. They were about four hundred metres away, so we drove toward them, with Patti and me mostly travelling, standing on the middle seat, head and shoulders out the top of the Land Rover. The bull started running toward us, with trunk raised and ears out, but Len kept on driving towards him, and the elephant kept on coming. Patti disappeared down below, while I was getting some good shots with my telephoto lens, but I hoped Len wasn't going to stall the vehicle when the bull was within a hundred metres of us. Len veered around and headed away, and soon after, the elephant pulled up, and then headed back to the others. Len said it was a sort of mock charge, but it looked pretty fair dinkum to us. Another pleasant camp in a watercourse area, with heaps of birds, but I tended to take more interest in the animal fauna.

There were a couple of interesting contrasts I could see between the African and Australian wildernesses. When it came to mass and variety of fauna, Africa is a clear winner. We hold our own very well with birds. The whole African continent has around fifteen hundred species, with the much smaller Australian continent containing half of that number. Most of the cockatoos are in Australia and South East Asia, plus we have a magnificent range of parrots. Africa only has several parrot species. However, the greatest contrast occurs in the form of isolation. There is any number of locations in Australia, where I can point my lead camel and travel in a straight line for over a thousand kilometres, without seeing another human being. Apart from a few areas of the Sahara, that is difficult to do in Africa, with growing numbers of people and cattle everywhere. We travelled on to Marsabit in northern Kenya, where we spent a day looking for Ahmed, but with no success.

On our way down to Samburu Park, we came across a small group of about a dozen Samburu people, clad in their red robes, and all carrying a lethal-looking, wide-bladed spear. They had cattle with them, which isn't unusual, because they are synonymous with cattle. They live mostly on cows' milk and cattle blood, which they tap from the cattle at regular intervals. No doubt, the odd goat and vegetables supplement that diet. They all ran up in great excitement, their only item of interest being Patti, who they kept referring to as "Mama", and after her initial apprehension, I think she quite enjoyed the attention. Half a dozen arms came through the window and touched her. Len and I felt quite out of it, while Jundy maintained an even lower profile in the rear, if that was possible.

We drove on to Samburu Lodge, where we enjoyed a luxurious evening, dining with numerous animals close by, and with excellent cuisine. The next day we spent some time in the park, filming lions, before heading back to Nairobi. It had been a very enjoyable African Safari, combining a whole range of experiences. It gave us a good idea of what could have been available, thirty or forty years ago. We were just happy that much of our trip was conducted outside of the park, something that will not be possible in the not too distant future.

Our last Kenyan highlight was a very touristy, but enjoyable experience. Freddie had organized a visit to Tree Tops, the famous African Safari Lodge, built in trees and overlooking a large waterhole. We travelled for several hours in a mini bus, finally arriving at a location in the bush, with a couple of huts. Here we were met by a white hunter-looking sort of bloke, complete with an elephant gun (.458 Winchester Magnum). There were half a dozen in our group, and he led us on this narrow walking track, through thick bush, for about twenty minutes, before we came to this huge clearing, in the middle of which was the Tree Tops complex. It was four o'clock in the afternoon, as we walked over to a set of steps at the bottom of the hotel, where we were met by two Africans, who escorted us about sixty feet up the steps. Tree Tops was like any other small, but well-appointed hotel, supported by huge wooden pylons, literally in the tops of a number of large trees. There were open viewing areas right around, mostly looking over the waterhole. Large floodlights remained on during the day, so that when darkness fell, there would be no sudden switching on of the lights, so disturbing the animals. At the moment, there was only a few species of antelope near the waterhole, with wild boars at the water, so we went into the cool interior, found our rooms and had a drink.

The most impressive thing about dinner was when three very black Africans, armed with three very white tablecloths, rolled in big bundles, came into the dining room. There were three tables, each about 14 metres long, and in unison, the men approached the tables and rolled the tablecloths onto them; very impressive, and obviously very practised. The meal was top notch, and half way through, we were instructed to go to our rooms to view a leopard on the waterhole. There was something of a stampede, and I hoped that the builders had done their job OK. We were just in time to see a leopard heading off, but not a good sighting by any means. After dinner, we viewed wildlife from on the top of the complex for a couple of hours, seeing some interesting interplay between elephant and buffalo. The African buffalo is one of Africa's most dangerous animals, which wasn't easily bluffed by the elephants.

We didn't get much sleep that night, waking up periodically, to see what was on the water, but I don't think anyone minded that. Next morning, after a sumptuous breakfast, we walked back with our man to the waiting mini bus, and drove back to Nairobi.

Millawe

With fond farewells to the Seeds and to Len Bennett, Patti and I took the relatively short flight south to Millawe, a small land-locked African country, landing at its capital, Blantyre. Travellers could be forgiven for thinking that they had landed in Sydney or similar. The place was all Gum trees and Holden cars. Our taxi was one of these, with a very enthusiastic African driver. In Kenya, I had been given the name of a hotel called The Blockhouse and asked the driver to take us there. He stopped the car and said, "Man, are you sure?" I told him yes, and with much shaking of his head, he drove us to this address on the outskirts of Blantyre. Patti and I stared at our destination. There and then, we should have changed our minds, but this name was fixed in my head as a recommended place to stay. The taxi driver drove off, still shaking his head, leaving us standing and staring at our night's accommodation. It consisted of a four-storey concrete blockhouse; the windows had no glass, and on the doubtful lawns surrounding the premises, lounged hundreds of Negroes. They all seemed to be looking at us, not so much hostile, but more in wonderment.

We picked up our gear and walked to a gash in the wall that I took to be reception, and in the gloom behind the concrete counter, I saw a pair of white eyes that gradually materialized into a face, as my eyes adjusted to the light. The little African was the manager, and sort of inquired whether we were sure that we wanted to stay here also. When I answered in the affirmative, he was obviously delighted, and led us up three flights of rough concrete stairs, to what I think was the penthouse or the honeymoon suite. En route, we passed many open doors, with Africans with transistor radios, lying on beds, many of them drinking. Our room at the end of the corridor was twice the size of those we had passed. Inside were two single beds, and a wardrobe with one door off, the other hanging off one hinge, plus a small table, and a mosquito net above our bed. It was as hot as an oven.

The manager left us, and the first thing we did was to push the wardrobe up against the door. Soon after, we realized that we had to purchase food, so away came the wardrobe, and with some trepidation, we left our gear in the room; except for our passports, as the door couldn't be locked. I wasn't game to leave Patti there on her own, or for her to go shopping on her own, so we didn't have much option. We spent an hour at a nearby market, buying fruit, and returned to our room, running the gauntlet of the assembly on the lawns.

With the wardrobe and table up against the door again, we were ready for a long night. Then there was a knock at the door. I yelled out "Who's there?" and the manager replied, saying that he had something for the "Mama." I guessed that was Patti, so once again we dragged the wardrobe away from the door. The little manager bloke was standing there with the biggest pineapple I had ever seen. He handed it to Patti, and we were both tickled pink. It really was a very generous act of friendship, and improved our day no end. The night sounded like an ongoing riot from behind our barricaded door, and we didn't sleep as well as we might have done.

Next morning we walked through what looked like a battle zone. A lot of sleeping black bodies, but those that were awake seemed friendly enough. When we reached the manager's hole in the wall, I thanked him for his kindness, and left him a paperback novel that I had with me, hoping he could read English. He rang another cab, which took us into the railway station at Blantyre. We were to travel into Mozambique, to the city of Beira on the coast, where we intended to spend a day, before travelling on to Zimbabwe. (Rhodesia, as it was then). We spent an hour in a long queue of Africans, before realizing that our travellers cheques were not going to be accepted. This meant spending another night in Blantyre, but there was no way it was going to be at the blockhouse. It turned out that this was a staging point for single Millawe men, travelling to work in the South African gold mines. We will never know why that was recommended to us.

After visiting a Barclays bank, we spent the night in a very clean comfortable hotel, not far from the railway station. After an early as possible breakfast, we headed down to the railway station, with an hour to spare. To our dismay, there was another massive queue, so we attached ourselves to the end. I could see the train, consisting of carriages that were not much better than cattle trucks, with glassless windows and hard benches to sit on. It was billed as a third class African train, and it was fast filling up. We could see that there was no way we were going to make it; there were people already on the roof, and we didn't reckon that was an option.

Then, a little African kid came up to us, telling me that we were to go up to the front of the queue. I declined, fearing we might be killed with sticks by an annoyed mob for jumping the queue. I could see the stationmaster beckoning us, and some of the crowd urged us to go, some even started clapping their hands. So off we went, feeling grateful, but also a bit guilty.

The smiling stationmaster sold us a ticket, and we boarded the train. This was the only train available, and it was something to be remembered. As far as I could see, we were the only whites, but we pushed our way through the mob and found a small gap on a bench near an open window. It was hot and the smells were interesting, to say the least.

It was about one hundred miles to the Mozambique border, and our information was that it would take a day, but in fact, it took two days. We noticed with interest that there were a number of soldiers on board, all armed with automatic weapons. The Rhodesian war was in its early stages, and they were, presumably guerrillas; I didn't like to ask.

The train travelled at a very sedate speed, with numerous stops. On some of these occasions, we purchased fresh fruit from people coming out of the bush. It was not comfortable travelling, but the people were friendly, and the scenery was interesting. The night was the worst, we had no option but to sit up all night and snatch what sleep we could, as the train rattled on toward the Mozambique border.

About mid morning on the following day, two white Americans came and sat near us. They were in their early twenties and they told us that they were draft dodgers. Shortly after, we pulled up at a small town, and they asked us to mind their rucksacks. We reluctantly agreed, while they headed off to get water. Half and hour later the train moved off, and they hadn't returned. I hoped they might have hopped on the rear of the train, but after a couple of hours they still hadn't turned up, and as far as we knew, their passports were in their rucksacks. We ended up leaving their gear at the next railway station, in the care of the stationmaster. We will never know how they got on. It put us in a tricky position, be we had to do something.

Late on the second day, the train reached the border. We were to transfer to another train here, and hoped that it was a better bet than the present one. There was another long queue, so we went over and joined it. Apparently, we had to present a visa to the Portuguese authorities; not good, we didn't have any. No one had told us about them, and I guess we were still a bit naïve about this travelling business. There was no option but to stay in the queue, and when I stood in front of the Portuguese army sergeant, I handed him my passport. He peered at it, then said "visa, visa, where is visa?" He wasn't happy as I pushed the passport back to him and said "Australian passport, very good", but to no avail. I turned around and told Patti that she had better have a go. She stepped forward, gave him a nice smile and asked him what seemed to be the problem. I had always heard that the Portuguese were better lovers than soldiers, and this bloke seemed to bear it out. Quickly, a change came over him; he gave an oily smile, but politely said we needed a visa. I had visions of being chucked into a Portuguese jail, so I whispered to Patti,

Trouble at the Border

"Offer him money." She asked if we could buy visas and his smile almost severed his head. It ended up costing us the equivalent of $40 Australian, for what could have cost us a couple of dollars in Blantyre. It was a relief to get away from there, and on to the relative luxury of the Portuguese train. We actually had a sleeper compartment, so we slept almost all the way to Beira, arriving just after breakfast.

We had a pleasant, lazy day here. A medium sized coastal city of white buildings, white beaches and blue sea. I have never swum in such warm water, and we were disappointed to find fist-sized globules of oil, here and there in the water. Not sure if this was a regular occurrence, or left from some earlier oil spill.

Mozambique - Rhodesia

The people here seemed to be a mixture of Africans, Portuguese and a large number of mixed race, Portuguese/African. We really didn't experience a lot of the Mozambique hinterland, because several hours after leaving Beira it was dark, and we enjoyed another sleeper on an excellent Rhodesian train. We awoke and had breakfast, just before we reached the Rhodesian border, and from then on, enjoyed the attractive countryside of Rhodesia (now Zimbabwe), a mixture of bush, savannah/bush and agriculture.

We were met by friends of friends in the capital, Salisbury (now Harare), a well-ordered, open attractive city, a bit smaller that Adelaide. After twenty minutes or so, we arrived at their house in the suburbs, where we were to spend a week. One of the main memories of this time was the Chameleons in the garden and house, with their ever-changing colour.

Next day we were interviewed by a journalist from the Main Rhodesian newspaper, on our Safari client swapping idea. Another day we spent with a Rhodesian Safari operator, at his place, with an afternoon in a nearby game reserve. This was a luxury operation, where newly arriving clients received violets and orchids on their pillows, the night prior to departure. All a bit full on I reckon, but I suppose their idea is to sweeten them up a bit before the trip. I think I would rather give them this treatment after the safari, in case they turned out to be a mob of bastards. Then, you would have the option of substituting the violets/orchids for Boxthorn or something similar!

Patti's father had been a rear gunner in the Lancasters, during the war, and was shot down over occupied France. He was captured by the Germans, and spent the last two years of the war in a German prisoner of war camp. While there, he had become good friends with a Rhodesian airman flying for the R.A.F. This man and his family ran a tobacco and maize farm in northern Rhodesia, and before we left Australia, Patti's father had written to his friend, saying that we would like to visit them when we arrived in Rhodesia; we had phoned him from Salisbury on arrival. Since our initial contact, the Rhodesian war had really escalated. My father in-law's friend said that, although they really wanted to see us, they simply were not willing to take the responsibility. However, they were prepared to have us for a day visit.

Consequently, leaving early one morning, Tim drove us up to the farm, near a town called Umvukwes, a three-hour drive from the city. It was a very interesting day, but we didn't envy the way they were living. The large bungalow style homestead had wire netting across all of the windows, to stop hand grenades being thrown through. There were three German Shepherd guard dogs in the house, and family members slept with a loaded revolver by their beds. You could cut the nervous tension with a knife, and we felt very sorry for them.

In the afternoon, the younger son took Patti and me for a drive around the farm, in a small Peugeot car. While driving through a maize plantation, the car had a flat tyre, and I have never seen anyone change a wheel so quickly. He was a blur, and I tried to help, but could have only slowed him down. After a few minutes, we were mobile again, as he explained that terrorists often laid up in the maize and tobacco during the day, coming out at night to raid the farms. There were several hundred Africans working on the farm, who appeared to be happy, but as time progressed, many of them were sympathizing with the guerrillas, so the owners didn't know whom they could trust. Driving back to Salisbury, we once again felt so very thankful that we were Australians.

Toward the end of our stay, we flew over the Victoria Falls, on the Rhodesian/Zambian borders, staying there overnight in a hotel. It is one of the natural wonders of the world, and viewing the falls almost defies description, and after an interesting evening in the old Grand Victoria Falls Hotel, we took a day launch trip up the Zambezi River, to a spot above the falls. As we took off, the thought passed through my mind, that it could be an interesting situation if the motor fails! We saw plenty of animal life on the banks, and had lunch on an island that seemed to have more than its fair share of monkeys. It was an achievement to eat your lunch without it being snatched from your hands. Back to the falls, and then we flew back to Salisbury.

It's interesting to note that, a month after Patti and I took the train from Blantyre to Beira, two carriages were derailed by an explosive device, set on the rails. No one was killed but there were some injuries. Three months after we returned home, the Zambezi launch was machine gunned from the Zambian side, by Rhodesian freedom fighters or terrorists. Two American girls were killed. A week after we travelled up to Umvukwes, to the tobacco farm, an Englishman was shot through the head during the day, so you just never know.

Our last week was spent in South Africa, and a very pleasant one it was. A mate of mine from Birdsville, David Brook, had flown over to South Africa a few weeks earlier, to see an old school-days pen friend, called Nell Schulenburg. They had met years ago in a school trip to Rome, and hit it off pretty well. A few letters followed, and then there was a long silence for a number of years. One day a photograph arrived in Brookie's mailbag, of an attractive South African airlines hostess, that turned out to be Nell. I was in Birdsville at the time and he showed me the photograph. Brookie's comment was, "I think I'll go and have a look at her," and that's exactly what he did. Needless to say, the trip was a good investment, and they have never looked back.

They invited Patti and me to stay with them in the capital, Pretoria. Nell's father is a surgeon, and we did a lot of driving around, visiting relations of hers who owned a winery at Stellenbosch, South Africa's famous wine region. South Africa is probably one of the world's most beautiful countries, and we were able to see a good bit of it. A short visit to Kruger Game Reserve and a couple of days, spent at Plettenbergbaai in Schullenburg's holiday house, was time well spent. David and Nella got married the same year, and have lived in Birdsville ever since, where they brought up their family.

A memorable day was spent on and around Table Mountain, a remarkable feature, where we went up and down in the famous cable car. Our second to last night was at a little nightclub in Cape Town. and at 3am, when the jazz combo played a jazz version of Waltzing Matilda, it bought tears to our eyes. We had been away for two and a half months, and were looking forward to returning to the Land of Oz. Our last night was spent in the big and dangerous city of Johannesburg, staying with a friend of Patti's parents; it was interesting, but not my favourite city.

A long flight from Jans Smuts Airport saw us in Perth, and when we walked outside, there were two things that filled me with nostalgia. One was the smell of the eucalypts, and the other was the sound of a crow calling.

10.

Willy Harris

I have an old Aboriginal mate in Birdsville called Willy Harris, who would now be in his late eighties, and in the thirty odd years that I've known him, his appearance doesn't seem to have changed a bit. He's one of the blackest black men that I've ever known, and I once photographed him white-washing the walls of the Birdsville pub. When I yelled out a greeting to him, he spun around and flashed a smile at me. His very white teeth and the freshly painted white wall contrasted dramatically with Willy's skin, thus producing a very memorable photograph.

A very hard worker was Willy, usually employed, either by the Diamantina Shire Council, or by Bill Brook from Adria Downs station. Willy had some interesting habits, one of which pertained to clothing. At the time, I think he was having some sort of a domestic problem, and getting his washing done was not one of his options. Determined not to do his own washing, Willy would walk into the Birdsville store (Which I was looking after at the time) to buy a set of R.M. Williams bush gear. Stockman cut strides, and a normally bright blue shirt that he would wear for about a week, before reappearing at the store to buy another set. This was one bold solution to his laundry problem, and I'm still unsure as to whether he had a stockpile of dirty washing, or if he just burnt them. I couldn't help thinking that it was a good job that he had steady employment.

Always happy and full of fun was Willy. I was in the store one day when Willy poked his head in through the doorway and said "Gooday." He was carrying a billy and a sugar bag full of something or other, and he had a mob of kids with him. It was a very hot day, as usual, so I asked him where he was going. "I'm going to boil the billy, and have a picnic for the kids" he said, "down under the big Coolibah at the end of the street." This Coolibah was just off the end of the newly bituminised main street of Birdsville, so I reckoned that this qualified as being in the country. Off he went with his tail of happy kids, nothing like the simple pleasures of life.

Willy was very much a "can do" sort of person, getting straight to the core of any problem. A good example of this was on one of my safaris into the Simpson Desert. This was during the time that I owned the Birdsville pub, and we used to operate a few safaris out to Lake Muncooney, a large fresh water lake, that often held water in the 1970s. We used an old six-wheel drive Studebaker truck, fitted with big aircraft tyres, to help it to negotiate the many high sand dunes west of Birdsville.

'Just Do It'

On this occasion, we were camped with a party on the edge of the lake, and Willy, turned out in brand new R.M. Williams clothing, was helping me to do some cooking. I asked one of the party members, a Melbourne bloke, to go and fill a billy from the lake. So he picked up a billy and walked down to the edge of the water. Willy was standing by the fire, watching this bloke, while I was cutting up some meat. He said to me, "that bloke's having a bit of trouble, Rex." He was too. As he stood on the edge of the water, gazing into the distance, his body language signalled frustration.

I immediately knew what his problem was, as there had been a westerly breeze blowing for the last day or two. This breeze had gently blown a large quantity of debris, including much cow dung, across to the eastern shoreline, near where we were camped. This debris had formed itself into a band, half a metre wide, around the edge of the lake, and our man's dilemma was that he couldn't reach across the dung belt to the clear water without getting his shoes wet.

Willy watched him for a while, before walking purposefully down to the lake and without a word, took the billy from the Melbournian's hand, and without breaking stride, strode out into the lake. This was one of the coolest things that I have ever seen. He kept on going until the water was up to his waist, filled the billy with nice clean water, then turned around and walked out again. He passed the astonished Melbourne bloke without acknowledgment, walked up and placed the billy on the fire.

The beauty of it all was that there was absolutely no thought of the grand gesture. The simple fact was that we required a billy full of clean water, and Willy went and got it. I didn't spoil the moment by making any comment; it was too priceless for that.

I saw Willy recently and he's still travelling well.

11.

Drama in the Air - Three Flights

In the last thirty odd years, I have done a lot of flying in light aircraft, as a passenger. I am not a nervous flyer, having flown many hours, with all manner of bush pilots. During that period, three occasions come particularly to mind.

Arnhemland

For years, we had a regular contract with a party of law people, Judges, Barristers, lawyers and their wives. On this occasion, we had to fly from Jabiru to Cobourg Peninsula in Arnhemland, where we had a base camp. We split up into three aircraft, one of them being a Piper Aztec, where passengers sat facing each other. I was sitting opposite a portly Barrister called Peter, and we were all jostling around putting on seat belts etc., prior to taking off.

We left the ground and soared up over the spectacular Arnhemland escarpment, and when we had been in the air about five minutes, the pilot levelled out for our short flight to Cobourg. All of a sudden, there was this very loud metallic banging noise, and I saw the pilot cringe in his seat. I'm sure the same thoughts raced through everyone's minds, - 'this is it, we're going down', or similar. The racket lasted for about five or six seconds and then went quiet. I could see the pilot looking out of his window, down the side of the aircraft, and then his body language showed that he was suddenly greatly relieved. Peter the Barrister's seat belt apparently, was the culprit! When he closed his door, the long end of his belt became jammed in the door, and when the plane reached a certain angle, the belt went mad, slapping the side of the plane. It took us all a while to settle down again, and enjoy the scenery.

Kimberley

We were spending a day, flying a party from Drysdale station, in the west Kimberley, out to the magnificent Kimberley coast, then back up the Prince Regent River, Mitchell Plateau to Drysdale. It involved three flights, taking five passengers each time. The pilot was not at all that familiar with this region, so I had accompanied the first flights, pointing out a few landmarks. The flights took about one and a half hours, and while that was happening, we had a camp back on the lovely Drysdale River, in a crocodile (salty) free area.

There was a spare seat on the final flight, and as no one else wished to go, I went along. When we took off, I heard an unusual clunking noise, not like the usual sound of the wheels folding up. I was sitting in the seat directly behind the pilot, who, it seemed to me, had suddenly become more agitated than usual. I had noted that he was one of those nervy pilots, all the time touching knobs and gauges, never just sitting there and flying. Soon after, he started talking on the radio, and although I couldn't hear him, he seemed to be conversing in an agitated manner. (On my first flight, he didn't use the radio, but he did point out the landmarks that he identified from his map). This time - not a word to the passengers.

I put two and two together, and came up with this scenario. The wheels had not folded up correctly, and he was talking to his base, desperately looking for a solution. He didn't want to alarm the passengers at this stage; everything seemed to point to this. Therefore, I sat in my seat, wishing like hell that I was anywhere but where I was. I was careful no to transfer my concerns to the party, but in addition to all this, the pilot seemed to be flying a slightly longer route than previously, and I thought, 'He is going to use up as much fuel as possible before a belly landing?' I had about an hour and twenty minutes to consider all this.

It went through my mind that this might be the last bit of Australia I was going to see, and although it was some of the most dramatically beautiful scenery in the country, I had no appreciation of it whatsoever. After a while, I took out my little green Dalgety notebook, and began writing a letter to Patti and the girls, including an update to my will; that's how serious I thought it was. When I had finished, I just sat there waiting for the pilot to warn the passengers of the impending crash landing.

We approached Drysdale station, and commenced our run in, but not a word from the pilot; He had only just finished on the radio, a non-stop effort for well over an hour. I was about to tap him on the shoulder, to ask him why he wasn't instructing the passengers in crash landing procedure, like putting your head on your knees etc., but something made me refrain from this. As we approached the strip, I braced myself, but felt the wheels touch normally, and we had an excellent landing. As we taxied over to the waiting Toyota, I couldn't make up my mind whether I was furious, or relieved, certainly a bit of both.

When we hopped out, I took the pilot aside for an explanation. He told me that the undercarriage on this aircraft would sometimes make that noise, and as for the radio, he said he had a mate who was flying in the area, and he'd spent all that time talking to him. He said that, as I was on board, he thought I would do the commentating. I was pretty well speechless, and I couldn't wait to get back to the camp for a beer. This was the hardest day's work I had done for a long time!

One of the most embarrassing times of my life

In 1998, I had to fly up to Birdsville, and I arrived out at Parafield Airport, near Adelaide, to take off at 6.30am. It is usually about a four-hour flight to Birdsville, so I made sure I visited the toilet prior to going on board.

The pilot was in his early twenties, and had never been up to Birdsville before. As we loaded, he asked if anyone wished to land at Leigh Creek airport for a toilet stop, everyone said no; well, they would wouldn't they?

There was another young bloke sitting next to the pilot, there were three attractive young females in their early twenties, and me, a relatively old buggar. We took off, heading north over South Australia's mid north farming country. I talked to the girl next to me for a while, but light aircraft are not conducive to deep and meaningful, so the conversation lapsed. I alternately read a book, and looked out the window. After a couple of hours, we were flying over the eastern side of the Flinders Ranges, when I suddenly received that sort of message that you don't want to receive in this situation. I needed a leak. 'It couldn't be,' I thought, not possible; I purposely didn't have any tea or coffee that morning. But, sure enough, I had the problem, and it wasn't going to go away. I willed it to 'go away', but it wouldn't, so I accepted the inevitable, unenviable situation.

I took out my little green notebook, and constructed a note to the pilot which read – "Dear pilot. I am busting. If this was an all-male flight, you could pass back the empty cool drink bottle, and Bob would be your uncle, however, that is not the case. Could you please land at Moolawatana?" I passed it over his shoulder and proceeded to watch his body language. I don't reckon that he'd ever received a note like that before, but his body was no indication of what was going on in his head.

After what seemed like an eternity, he suddenly passed back an empty cool drink bottle! You could have knocked me over with a feather, I wanted to shrink up and disappear; but that was no escape; I had a problem and I had to deal with it.

I yelled at the young lady next to me, because you have to in a light aircraft, telling her that I needed to use the bottle. She stared at me, a look of horror on her face. I said, "Don't worry, I've got a blanket here that we can rig up." Eventually I had found one under the seat, and it was the only thing going for me at the moment. The two girls in the back weren't quite in the picture, as they couldn't hear what was going on. All they could see was the expression on the other girl's face, and me trying to rig up a blanket, a very strange state of affairs. I had to get the girl sitting next to me, and one of the girls in the back, to hold up one end of the blanket. They were now viewing me in a very strange way. I was finally set up as well as I was going to be, while the pilot and the other bloke in the front seat, were staring straight ahead, wanting no involvement with this aerial drama. I then started to get organized with the bottle, and If you think that's an easy enough task, think again. For a start, you sit hunched up in a light aircraft, with about as much room between you and the next passenger to put an envelope.

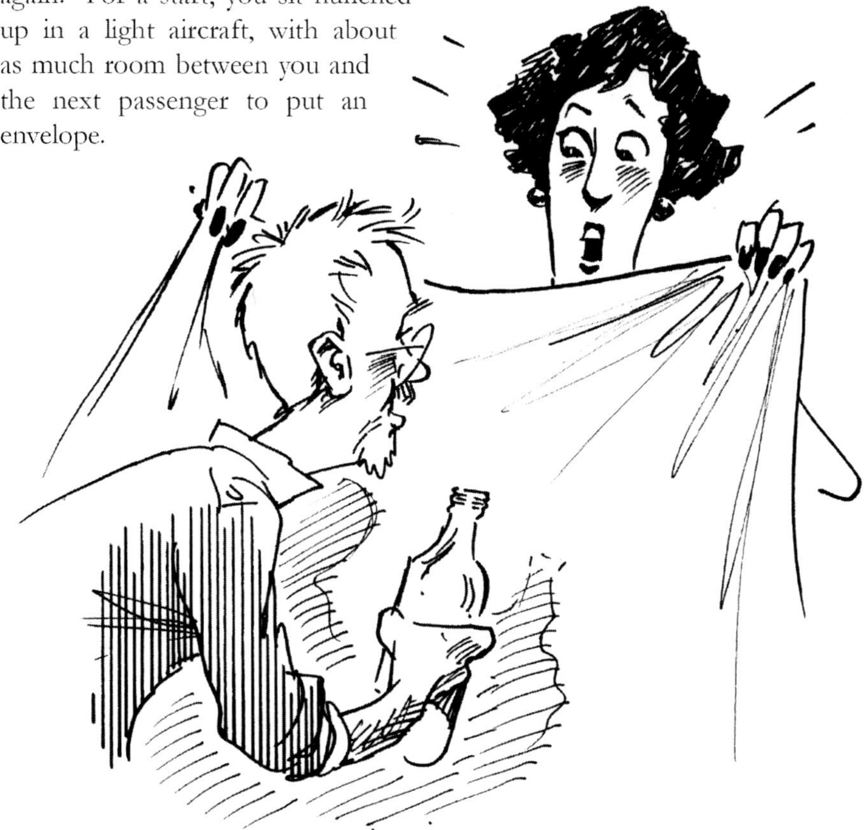

Exposure Above the Desert

Anyway, I finally had the bottle in place and proceeded to do what I had to do, but to my horror, nothing happened; well, hardly anything. There was no fear of overflowing the bottle, and I thought, 'How could this be?' What had been only a bad dream, was turning into my worst nightmare. I waited for about five minutes, but that was definitely it. Just then, the girl next to me, thinking I must have long since completed my task, dropped the blanket. She gave a shriek that made me almost drop the bottle, before she disappeared behind the blanket again. Do you have any idea how I felt? Well, I finally sorted myself out, put the top on the bottle and placed it under my seat. I then scratched on the blanket that was cautiously lowered.

Three pairs of eyes bored into me, and if I didn't feel a second class citizen before, I certainly did now. I sort of tried to make a joke of it, but that fell as flat as the desert that was now passing below us. So I retreated into my book, at least grateful that the drama was over; but it bloody well wasn't. Twenty minutes later, I had the same problem again. Well, I knew one thing for sure; rather than go through that performance again, I would have broken the window and jumped out, so I began playing mind games as I read my book, willing myself to think of everything but my problem. It worked for a while, but I was losing the game. I kept looking out of the window for a landmark so I could pace myself, but we were flying over featureless desert country, and I recognized nothing; but suddenly I did. I saw a watercourse that runs into the Diamantina River, and I now knew we were only ten minutes away from Birdsville. There had been a strong head wind on this flight, and it was taking longer than it had before. I was in agony, but they reckon you can put up with anything for ten minutes. The atmosphere in the plane had changed since my performance; I reckon I was viewed as the 'dirty old man', which wasn't a very nice feeling. I felt like assaulting the pilot with a part filled cool drink bottle, but it was my very own problem. When we approached Birdsville, the pilot started flying this gigantic circle, so wide that I could almost see Alice Springs - well almost. 'Put the bloody thing down' I said to his head, but he was playing it very much by the book.

You might think my troubles were over when we hit the deck; well you'd be wrong there, as today the pub was closed. There used to be an outside toilet when I owned it, but the whole show had been sanitized, and the only loo within my very limited range, was at the motel. I scuttled across the tarmac like a wounded crab, and homed in on room number 7, a lucky number I hoped. There were people everywhere, and cover was scarce, but I knocked on the door. - No answer, so holding my breath (and other elements), I opened the door and walked in, conscious of the risks I was taking. My credibility had already taken a body blow today, and I wasn't looking for a double whammy. No one about, but clothing was laid out on the bed. Like a heat-seeking missile, I dived for the loo, where I spent what seemed like about ten minutes. I didn't spend a penny, I spent my life savings, and If the occupiers of the room had come in, I had no idea what I was going to say, but finally I emerged from the room.

I almost perished in Birdsville that day. Because I had to fly back again that evening, I hardly had a drop of anything to drink, and it was a hot spring day. The flight back was uneventful, and I reckon they must have drawn straws to see who was going to sit next to me.

12.

Four Legged Mates

It's a dull life in the bush without a dog, and I have had my fair share over the years. As a kid, our first family dog was a Wire-haired Terrier who killed sheep, so had to disappear. A nice mongrel representing many breeds replaced him, but I forget what happened to him. After that, I had a brown and white Whippet who was a great character and his name was Jock.

At that time, I lived with my Dad and Mum in McLaren Vale, on the edge of the town near the railway station, and Jock used to have a town run, visiting various places where he would get a regular handout. The best for him was the butcher shop, operated by my uncle Lloyd, with my cousins John and Jim; I can still see him dragging a massive bone down Field Street to our house. I often used to go hunting with Jock, chasing rabbits, hares and foxes. Jock lived to a ripe old age and then I had a gap for a couple of years, without a dog, because I went to a boarding school in Adelaide. Then, when I went jackerooing in 1960, I had a Kelpie/Collie cross as my first sheep dog. He was a nice dog, but not much of a worker, which was probably due to my lack of experience.

During my time of jackerooing in the South East, I acquired two small Kelpies, Kylie and Tibun, red and black respectively. These I took to Lake Everard station in the north west of South Australia. I had learnt a lot about working dogs, from John Wilkinson in the southeast, and these dogs were of great use with big mobs of sheep; they were also great mates. I lost Kylie after a few years, but Tibun lived to a ripe old age. She often preformed her special trick when we were at the beaches and I had time off from the station. I could point to a vehicle with an open window, with or without people in it, and I'd say "jump up in the bus", and she would race off and spear straight through the window, virtually causing mayhem in the car. I had to choose my mark carefully, as one bloke was outraged and wanted to fight me, but I just told him that I didn't know what got into Tibun. I said she had never done anything like that before, which sort of calmed him down after awhile. He had a girl with him, and I think proceedings may have been at a delicate stage. When I went into the Safari business, I traded Tibun for a wife, leaving her (Tibun) at Mt Serle station in the Flinders Ranges.

My next dog was a Doberman bitch called Nari, a great character, who rode around Australia on top of my 4 x 4 International. Unfortunately, I ran over her when she was five years old, and that was a black day. Another Doberman dog that I owned, wasn't a great success so I gave him away.

Then came a blue heeler called Mincka, who had quite an illustrious career. There were quite a lot of incidents, even when I went to inquire about a Blue Heeler pup, at a farm at Echunga in the Adelaide Hills. I went around the back of the homestead to knock on the door and, sitting near the door was a sharp looking Red Kelpie, just sitting there without moving a hair. I said "How are you going bloke' and went to knock on the door. I hesitated, because there was something funny about the Kelpie. That sure was an understatement, because the bloody thing was stuffed, complete with two glass eyes; an interesting concept I thought and it turned out that this had been a much-loved dog. Depends on your point of view, but I think I would rather bury my dogs and retain their memories.

Right from a pup, I took Mincka on the camel trips, where he had a pretty diverse set of experiences. One trip, I was coming down from the Petermann Ranges to the Mann Ranges, in the extreme north west of South Australia. He used to sleep on top of a packsaddle, in the groove, on a saddle blanket.

Running with a 'Baton'

We were experiencing very cold nights on this trip, with icy mornings. This particular morning the billies were frozen over before sunrise and our swags were covered in frost. I walked over to where Mincka was camped, and saw a sort of white cone poking up out of the saddle, at an angle of 45°; it was Mincka's nose! His rear end had gradually subsided into the opening of the saddle, leaving just his nose sticking out and it was covered with frost! His eyes were half open and, for a minute, I thought he had frozen to death! I poked him in the eye and he blinked so he was okay. He gradually got out of bed and creaked around on a very stiff set of shanks.

Mincka was a bluey without a killer instinct, so when we came across dingoes in the Simpson Desert that had no contact with humans, he would initially chase them, but they mostly didn't run, and he just bounced off them, sometimes both of them falling over. He would get up, shake his head in disgust and trot back to us. Probably the most extraordinary think that happened concerning Mincka, or any other dog for that matter, occurred before sunrise one day south of Oodnadatta. I wandered away from camp to attend to my toilet, with Mincka running around picking up sticks like he usually does. Now I don't want to offend the more sensitive, but what I am about to relate actually happened; even though I still find it hard to believe. I scratched out a hole in the ground, and settled down to do what billions do every day. It was underway as it were, when I suddenly experienced a vigorous buffeting in that area. Mincka flew past, clutching the 'object' in his mouth and I just couldn't believe it. I felt sort of deprived, yet amused at the same time, and went back to the camp. Bill and Fred didn't believe me at first but, when they saw the clean up job that Mincka needed, well - they believed it then.

When I lived on Kangaroo Island, my eldest daughter, Georgi, who was 7 years old at the time, wanted a puppy. I had long considered Bull Terriers, so I went over to the mainland to pick up a red and white bitch, about six months old, that we called Nosepeg. The name pertained to the wooden peg in a camel's nose, but later it had other connotations! Georgi was devastated when she saw how big the pup was, expecting a cuddly little handful. Nosepeg became a great character, often accompanying me across Backstairs Passage on board Emu Air. This small airline allowed the carrying of animals and many a tale is told of happenings on board. This was where Nosepeg became an acute embarrassment. She would wait until we were well under way, before releasing one of her devastating "silent sneakers". The first time, I just huddled down in my seat and wore the accusing looks of fellow passengers. However, next time (she did it every time, even with nothing to eat the night before), I just turned around, looked toward the rear of the aircraft and tried to shift the blame; this ploy worked well. Bull Terriers, though, seem to have no conception of pain or discomfort, and Nosepeg would often ride in the cabs of my Blitz Truck, people carrier, sprawled over the low range and winch levers. On several occasions, we had to stop the truck and vacate in a hurry due to one of her "bombs".

She would travel on the camel trips, riding on the packsaddles, tied by a short rope. Now and then, someone would yell out "Nosepeg's hanging." This was never an immediate problem, due to Bully's having necks like stobie poles (an infamous South Australian electric light pole built from concrete and steel), she would dangle happily for five minutes or so if necessary.

At the same time, I had a white Bull Terrier dog called Bundy Rum which, unfortunately, I bought sight unseen, after he'd travelled across to Adelaide in a semi-trailer's tool box. I thought he would be in the cab, but apparently, the truckie didn't like dog hairs on his seat. Consequently he was somewhat traumatized when he arrived, so it took some months to get him right. He and Nosepeg used to have some shocking fights, impossible to break up, unless you could manage to get them both underwater. I tried everything, even the old bush trick of a pair of pliers on the ear but, when I'd earmarked him, I gave up on that one. After a while, I would let them go. They didn't do much damage to each other, and would fight themselves to exhaustion, often going to sleep with their mouths still latched on.

One very interesting thing happened concerning Bundy Rum. I was doing a one-day camel trek through the Ravine de Casoars,

'Nosepeg' on the nose

up on the 800-foot cliffs at the back of our farm, when Bundy decided to tag along, under a camel called Pelican who kicked the shit out of him. Bundy came flying out and took off into the bush. I waited for a while, calling him, but he didn't return, so I went on, leaving my coat there. Often a dog will return and camp by an object of its owner. On my return, he wasn't there and I thought he might have gone home, however, that wasn't the case. I rang the couple of neighbours that we had down there, plus the lighthouse at Cape Borda, to ask them if they'd keep an eye open. I walked and rode for miles along the tracks, but not a sign of Bundy Rum so, after a few weeks, we wrote him off.

Christmas was upon us and, on Christmas morning, I got out of bed to put the kettle on. As I walked into the living room, I saw the tips of what looked like two white ears protruding above the screen door. I went to the door and, asleep on the doormat was Bundy Rum. What a Christmas present! The family all headed out of their beds and what a fuss we made of him, even Nosepeg nearly wagged her tail off. The surprising thing was that his condition was brilliant. He must have been living off possums, which are very terrestrial on Kangaroo Island, and the Tammar wallabies that were as thick as fleas on a dog. It was quite a homecoming.

In the mid nineties, I acquired my first Jack Russell Terrier and, as far I am concerned, I will not move from that breed. They are a "dog for all seasons", totally devoted, loyal, scared of nothing (which can be a problem) and with unlimited energy. Jack Russells are a very clean breed, making them ideal as housedogs, and life is never dull with one of them. They are small, and easy to carry in or on a vehicle, animal or boat. They make excellent watchdogs and, for small dogs, they come equipped with formidable sets of teeth. Two Jack Russells can clean up any other large dog, because they are not particular what they grab hold of. Dedicated hunters, they need careful monitoring in this area.

I called this pup Trouble, which proved to be very apt. We only had him for a bit over two years, but he lived for every second of that time. Right from the start, I took him on the Safaris, where he travelled on vehicles, camels, boats and our large Murray River raft (the Magic Carpet). He had many adventures and I'll relate several of them here.

On one occasion, we were doing a camel trek in the Flinders Ranges, walking along this Gum Creek with Trouble running along in front and to the side of the string. They have this ability to run fast with their nose inches from the ground, like a vacuum cleaner, following scents. He shot across the creek in front of the camels, and disappeared over the bank. I asked Patti, who was on the camel behind me, if she had seen where he went, but she hadn't, but I soon recognised our location. There was an old copper mine nearby, a vertical shaft of about 14 metres so, with some foreboding, I sat the camel down, hopped off and ran up over the bank. My worst fears being realized for sure enough, he had speared straight into the mine, which was immediately over the bank. I called his name and, to my great relief, Trouble let out a bark. If he had howled, I would have been more concerned, as that could mean he was injured; I could just see him down there.

We rigged up a rope, tying it to a Black Oak tree, a few feet from the edge of the mine. I took a sheepskin off one of the saddles and put it over my head to protect me from falling rocks, and then I descended. When I got down about six metres, the walls were timbered and the going was easier. I arrived at the bottom to find him as good as gold, with just a small scratch on one side. His momentum had taken him across the top of the mine, where he probably hit the far side, breaking his fall somewhat. The bottom of the mine, being damp earth, had also helped. Still, it was remarkable that he was uninjured. He jumped up on me, pretty pleased about my arrival, so I put him in a sugar bag, tied it carefully, and he was pulled up to the top, where he straight away headed off again, nose to the ground. I, on the other hand, spent ten minutes scratching my way up out of the mine, arriving at the top as if I had just finished a five-kilometre run. I hoped Trouble wasn't going to make a practice of quick, deep descents.

Rabbit burrows, on the other hand, were not as dangerous, although snakes in burrows were always a worry. He would go down any burrow and often kill rabbits, but never bring them up. Sometimes he would spend more than an hour underground, often re-appearing to see if we were still waiting. Then, the little bugger would go back down again for another session. Travelling across the rabbit-infested Strzelecki Desert by camel gave him plenty of scope. Lunch usually lasted for an hour, and as soon as we stopped, he would be straight down the nearest warren for the whole period. However, as soon as the camels jumped to their feet, he would pop out of the warren like a prairie dog. Didn't like the idea of being left behind.

Another time we were on a 4WD trip, camped on the Cooper, south of Longreach. In the party was D'arry Osborn, a wine maker friend of mine, who is a very keen angler. He was fishing for Yellow Belly in the Cooper one evening and was half way through his cast, with the rod behind his head and sinker and hooks behind him. As he went to launch his line into the river, there was a great series of howls from Trouble. He had taken and half swallowed the bait, so I grabbed him and saw the hook well down his gullet. I tried to extract it with a pair of long nosed pliers, but to no avail. I then did what turned out to be a dangerous thing; I cut the line as close to the hook as possible. It was a long night with Trouble camped by our swag, in a very agitated state, obviously uncomfortable with the hook inside him. I intended to call on the radio in the morning to make a rad-phone call to a vet for advice. Trouble kept moving around all night. In the morning, before the RFDS opened, Trouble suddenly arched his back, gave a large cough, and out flew the hook with the bait still attached. What a relief for all concerned, and D'arry was particularly relieved. I learnt later that, if you cannot extract the hook, then you should cut the line and leave about six inches to act as a 'tail'. This allows the hook to go through, without rotating and tearing the stomach lining. Trouble definitely used up one of his lives then.

It was on this trip that Trouble's musical career was launched. We decided to walk into Combo waterhole (where Banjo Patterson wrote 'Waltzing Matilda'), one morning before sunrise, and took along the billy and the tea. We boiled the billy and, in a frivolous frame of mind, acted out the song. I jumped into the waterhole and jumped out again pretty quick, because it was very cold. While we drank our tea, I picked up a mouth organ and started to play Waltzing Matilda. Straightaway Trouble sat up, like the dog logo of His Masters Voice fame, and began the mournful howling. As the song progressed, he varied his howling, so it was all very entertaining for the listeners. This became a regular gig of ours on trips. I trained Trouble to accompany me into pubs, when I'd wrap him up in a coat or pullover and walk inside with him under my arm, where he would then lie motionless, wrapped up on my knees under the table. There were probably times when he wished that his master was a teetotaller.

After I'd had him for a year or so, I purchased another female Jack Russell pup, one who had already had her tail docked (Like a growing number of people, I do not believe in docking tails). We called her Minnie, and she was a great little dog. Soon she was in pup to Trouble and eventually, she gave birth to two females that we temporarily called Big and Little, until we could think of permanent names for them. When they were only twelve days old, I ran over Minnie and, as anyone who loves dogs would know, it was a terrible day. Patti then had to rear the pups on bottles. When the pups were only six months old, Little chased a brown snake under a tarp that was covering some timber. She was bitten on the nose and she died within minutes. Bigger remained Bigger, sometimes shortened to Biggy, and we still have her. She is very much Patti's dog, and is her loyal companion when I am away on bush trips.

Jack Russells are compulsive snake killers, and Trouble killed his fair share. He would spend an hour shaking them after they were dead. One summer evening there was a commotion in our back yard and, when we went out, there was a dead Brown Snake less than a metre long. As we watched, Trouble gave a little stagger and with dread we realized that he'd been bitten. The Common Brown Snake is the second deadliest snake in the world; so few dogs have survived their bites. I rang Phil Hutt, a veterinarian mate of mine in Berri, but there was no time to try anti venom. I had heard that massive doses of vitamins can save animals from snakebite, and I kept syringes full of it in the fridge. Phil said that there was no scientific reason why it should work, but there was no harm in trying. He also told me of an old wives tale about immersing a dog in cold water, with just the head clear. I did this in the laundry tub, for twenty minutes, and although he looked sick, he hung on. When I took him out, I put him on a blanket; he seemed to want to keep moving. He was obviously in pain, but was still alive more than half an hour after the bite. I started to hope that all was going to be OK, but soon after, he began passing blood and died. We were heart broken; I had been closer to him than any other dog. We buried him out the back with Minnie and Little under a big old Mallee tree.

Soon after, Bigger had Troubles pups, three in number, a male and two females. We called the male Stubbie, and the two females, Weetbix and Yak. We sold Yak, keeping Weetbix and Stubbie, and Stubbie became my bush mate, or my 'going away' dog, in place of Trouble. He looked similar to Trouble except that he had one white eye and, very early in the piece, he became a little character. Sometimes the three dogs, Bigger, Weetbix and Stubbie, would get out of the back yard compound, if a gate was left open, and would disappear hunting, often for the day. We live on Mallee-covered cliffs on the River Murray, upstream from Morgan, and the dogs were brought up on these cliffs so they know every hole and crevice. On one occasion, Stubbie and Weetbix got out of their compound and were away for the day. Weetbix arrived back at dusk, but no sign of Stubbie, which was very unusual. I hopped in the car and drove out the gate to see if I could see him. There he was limping through the gate dragging a broken foot and his head covered in blood. I put him by the fireside and Patti patched him up as well as she could; there was a large flap of skin hanging off his head. Next day she took him into Phil, at his practice in Waikerie, to get him treated. Stubbie returned with a plastic tube, a couple of inches long, sticking out of the top of his head, just like a periscope. He looked a real dag, but this was to drain the head injury. A Jack Russell can't be restrained and he would race around, all over the place, with his "periscope". But Phil had done a good job and Stubbie survived with hardly a mark on him. The peculiar thing resulting from this accident, (we reckoned he had been hit by a semi-trailer), was that, as we travel along in a vehicle, with him sitting up and looking out of the front window, he ducks down below the dash board whenever he sees a grid or an approaching semi-trailer. He is still doing that, nearly five years after the accident, so it must have made a lasting impression on him.

I was playing Waltzing Matilda on the mouth organ one day, when he jumped up on the table and howled like a beauty; however, the difference between him and Trouble is very marked. Trouble never shifted from the "His Masters Voice" stance, but Stubbie is more like the entertainer, Peter Allen. Totally unpredictable, he will sometimes emulate Trouble, but at other times, will hop up on to someone's knee and howl; or on or under a table. Sometimes he will do it lying down. For all this, the gig is no less entertaining. Stubbie has one physical trait that I have seen in no other dog, and it is his tree climbing ability. If a tree is climbable, he is up it. I have seen him as high as fifty feet, and we would worry about him falling, but he never looks like it. The nearest he ever came to grief, was once in the Flinders Ranges. We were travelling up a gully on camels, when I heard him bark and saw him over twenty feet high in a Mulga tree, and about five feet above him was a huge tabby cat. I stopped the string, took my 30-30 Winchester rifle out of its scabbard and shot the cat, causing it to drop like a stone, almost knocking Stubbie off his branch. He seemed to duck out of the way and then scampered down to inspect the dead cat. At times he goes into a sort of trance, and creeps slowly around items of furniture in a weird manner. I have heard of other dogs doing this, but have never found out the reason for it.

Lastly, I will relate someone else's story of a Jack Russell, to illustrate their total dedication to getting a job done. A mate of mine has one that he took out rabbiting one day. They were waiting for ages for the dog to come out of a rabbit burrow, when finally they saw the odd puff of dust and heard periodic grunts. Eventually the tip of his tail appeared, and Jack could tell he that was straining himself to the max. Then a bit more of his tail appeared, then his hindquarters, muscles rippling. Then the whole of him emerged and he had a fox by the "Family Jewels" – he had long since lost interest in any feeling.

Note: In August 2004, Stubbie was stolen from our property while Patti and I were running an ornithological trip in Queensland. I managed to get some publicity on this, and sent posters all over the state. Had some encouraging reports of sightings, but no success. Maybe I will get him back.

In the meantime his job has been taken over by a three month old Jack Russell Male called 'Billycan'. He's showing a lot of promise.

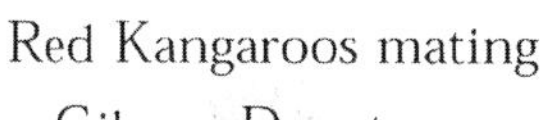

Red Kangaroos mating
– Gibson Desert

Zebra Finch caught
in Orb Spider web
– Great Sandy Desert

Ooldea Mallee
(Euc. Youngiana)
– Great Victoria Desert

A Numbat

Victoria
Desert Camels

Negotiating sand
dune country

4-Legged Mates

A bagged dog

Swimming the Cooper

An Outback Waterhole

In a Sea of Sandhills

Lunch camp. Fiona Wallace in charge.

Remains of Old Aboriginal Wurlies

Stavros Pippos with old water canteen from the 1902 Maurice expedition

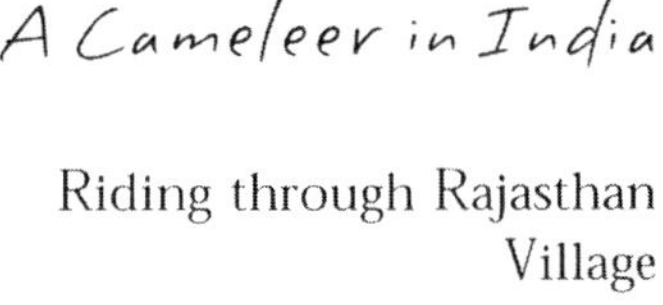

A Cameleer in India

Riding through Rajasthan Village

I Will Not Complain

Japanese party on raft

Spuds and Water

Broken down on the Nullarbor

The Buggered Bustard

13.

Swimming the Cooper

It was a wet year inland and we were following the Cooper down in flood; our transport was camels. The country had received excellent local rains, and was in wonderful heart, with the sand difficult to see for wildflowers. Poached eggs were the dominant species but others, including Bacon and Eggs, Wild Parsnip and Yellow Bud, covered many of the flood flats where the water had receded.

As well as chasing wildlife, one of the other objectives of this expedition was to try to locate a cache of gear, buried long ago by the explorer, John McKinlay. To our knowledge, this had never been recovered so we were very optimistic about our chances, as we had the location coordinates. As we approached the site however, it became obvious that we would somehow have to get across a channel of the Cooper. Aware of this fact, we decided to make camp, on this particular afternoon, on the banks of the creek. It was the usual excellent Cooper camp, with abundant feed for the camels, big Coolibahs supplying deep shade, and some of the best firewood in the world; and of course, this year there was more water than you could poke a stick at. We decided then that we should make this our base camp for two nights.

According to our information, the McKinlay location was only four kilometres from our camp, but there was no way that we'd be able to get the camels across to the other side, as the channel was too deep and the water running too swiftly. Our decision then was that we'd have to swim across, a distance of about 140 metres, and then walk to the location of the buried equipment. I have a great respect for rivers, especially when they're running at this speed. I swam across the main channel of the Cooper, on the Birdsville Track, in 1974, an action that taught me this respect. I had to start well upstream from the place where I intended to land, using the current to assist me, rather than fighting it by trying to swim straight across.

The next day, after much discussion, we decided that four of us would make the swim across the Cooper. There was Graham, a cameleer, Tony, one of the expedition members, my nine year old daughter Kate, and me. I knew that three of us were strong swimmers, but I was unsure about Tony's ability. He assured me however, that he was a strong swimmer, and was dead set on going, having a keen interest in our mission. I was well aware of the potential dangers, and even though Kate could swim like a fish, I made a mental note not to tell her mother. (She eventually found out). In preparation, we took four sheets of plastic, approximately three metres long by nearly two and a half metres wide, upon which we placed our boots, clothes and necessary gear. We brought the sides together and tied them up, so that the end result somewhat resembled Christmas puddings; and they floated very well.

We entered the water near our camp, with the rest of the party eagerly looking on. This was July, and even though the daytime temperatures were around 25^{0}C, the water felt very cold. We arranged to swim line abreast, pushing our 'Christmas puddings' in front of us, using them for floatation when necessary. As the water became deeper, the current soon made its presence felt, so we could anticipate being swept a long way downstream. We kept on swimming steadily, but I noticed that Tony seemed to be making hard work of it. He was making for a snag that stuck up, about two thirds of the way across, and on reaching it, he latched on to it like a heat-seeking missile. After a while, he waved us on, and five minutes later, we reached the bank on the far side. Soon after, Tony let go of his snag, and started out in our direction. Graham and I swam out to help him, guiding him towards land. He seemed to be pretty well buggered, because his Christmas pudding had developed a leak and was taking on water; we opened it up and discovered a couple of small holes in the plastic.

After sorting ourselves out, we headed off on our course, making for a sandhill some half a kilometre away. However, upon reaching the top of the ridge, we were dismayed to see a sheet of water, stretching all the way to the horizon. It was that sort of a flood, and there was no guarantee that we could locate our target, especially with the daylight that we had left. Reluctantly we turned and retraced our path, back to the Cooper channel. I must say here, that I was more than a little concerned for Tony, realising that he was anything but a strong swimmer. We incorporated his load into Graham's and mine, and then we put him and Kate in the middle, between Graham and me. He was able to make use of our bundles, if he needed a spell, and we agreed to stick together in a group.

We set off OK, but as we neared the middle of the stream, the current, now much stronger than before, took hold of us. We kept on swimming steadily, apart from a couple of minutes when Tony needed a spell, and clung on to a bundle. I could see our camp fast disappearing, and what concerned me most was the very real possibility of us being swept out onto a huge flat.

The current for some reason was now very definitely stronger on this return swim. Our camp was situated on the top end of a long sand spit that ran out onto this flat, and had a small, stunted River Coobah on the end of it. Although we were going with the current, we started working towards that little tree; it suddenly assumed a great importance.

If we were unable to land upstream of this tree, then we were going to be swept out onto the large flood flat. My concern now was that, if the water there was deep, (judging by the look of a few flooded Coolibahs, its depth was about one and a half metres), we could have difficulty getting in, and the next stop could be the Birdsville Track. After a worrying, fifteen minute swim, I could see that we were in fact going to make it. Eventually we managed to drag ourselves ashore, fit for nothing but a ten-minute lie down on the sand. Before we returned to the camp, about one kilometre away, I went over and gave that little Coobah an affectionate pat.

14.

The Sydney Push

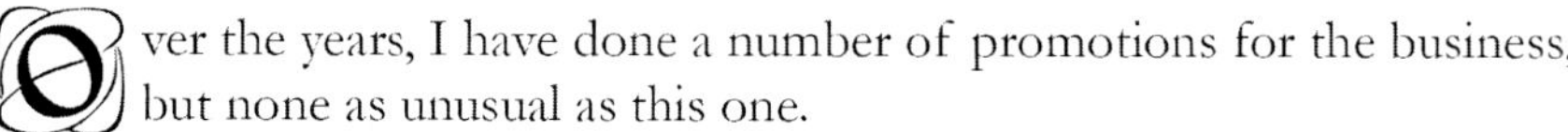

Over the years, I have done a number of promotions for the business, but none as unusual as this one.

In the mid 1980s, one of the owners of the Sydney Centre Point Tower did one of our camel treks in the Flinders Ranges, and became very enthusiastic about camels. Some months later she phoned, explaining a promotion of theirs with an outback flavour. The main theme was that, if all the cables that held up the Centre Point Tower were unravelled, the individual strands joined together would stretch all the way to Ayers Rock. Well, no one would argue with that.

She then asked me if I would bring a complete 'camel camp' over to Sydney, including a camel. All expenses would be paid, and my company would get some excellent, high profile publicity. I managed to talk her out of including the camel, as it was a big expense, and would not have been kind to the camel. It was therefore arranged to hire a camel from Bullen's Circus.

My brief was to bring one of everything that I would normally have in a camel camp. It was the best proposition that I had received for ages, and I looked forward to it. A few days before the event, I assembled some very unlikely 'luggage'. It included my swag, a pack saddle, a riding saddle, a pair of pack bags (later to be stuffed with paper), saddle bags, radio transceiver with aerial, a .375 Winchester rifle, maps, compass, water canteens, billies, camp oven, wok and a few smaller items.

On the day before I was due to leave, the gear was loaded onto my Toyota, at our depot at McLaren Flat. I drove down to the Ansett Freight depot at the Adelaide airport, and what might have been just a routine day for the freight blokes, suddenly brightened up. First, they thought I was some sort of nut, but soon realised that I was fair dinkum. I told them that it was imperative that the gear was on the same flight as me, having nasty thoughts about me arriving in Sydney with my artefacts circumnavigating the country, but they laughingly assured me that all would be well.

The next day, my sister Dianne, drove me from her place, where I had spent the night, to the airport. On the flight to Sydney, I had the thought that it was probably a pretty rare occasion for a camel packsaddle to be travelling at 30,000 feet above terra firma.

I was met at the Sydney airport by an old bushy that turned out to be the odd jobs/handyman attached to the Centre Point Tower. He was, however, driving a vehicle that was totally inadequate for the pick-up job. It was an old FE Holden station wagon, with a funny little roof rack. Working on the old adage that 'nothing is impossible', we finally loaded the last item. The load on the roof rack, dominated by the large packsaddle, was as high again as the Holden, and it attracted quite a few curious stares as we drove through the city.

We eventually arrived at a location above the Harbour called Castlecrag that was a picnic area, surrounded by bush, and running all the way down to the sea. The temperature was nudging the ton, and my earlier concerns regarding bushfires resurfaced. I had to build a large campfire, so at this stage, I decided that I'd better explain what I had been imported here for.

Part of the Centre Point Tower/outback promotion included a competition cook-up, between the Centre Point restaurant's head chef and me. About fifty assorted media were to be invited, and they were to vote on the tucker. I was to spend about an hour on my camp cooking, before a camel would be delivered, followed by the media. I was to give a few rides, then tell a couple of stories, while I finished cooking and serving the tucker. A very busy bloke I would be.

It was already 10am, and I was having nightmares about bushfires. When I had raised the matter earlier, my Centre Point friend told me not to worry about it, she would handle it. Well, I knew she had a lot of clout, but populations get very funny about being burned out. I had been involved in plenty of bushfires, and wasn't happy about the situation. No expense was being spared, so I asked the odd jobs bloke to go to the nearest merchandise store, and buy me three sheets of corrugated iron and some small steel posts. I explained that I wasn't about to settle at Castlecrag, but he seemed a little perplexed when he headed off.

I found a bit of a 'camp' to set up my site, ignoring the manicured barbecue areas, as my system would not have fitted in with them. The Holden duly returned with the iron and steel on the roof rack. This was dropped off, and the odd jobs bloke then retreated to some less demanding situation. I made a three-sided wind break with the iron and droppers, so I lit up my wood heap. I had brought along my own firewood (Coolibah), as I didn't trust the unknown (to me) timber around the Harbour. I required the very best coals because, you might say, I was cooking under pressure. This was important business, with a huge potential for a major stuff-up.

While the fire burnt down, I put the finishing touches to my 'camp'. I then mixed up a damper, and placed it in the camp oven, ready to bury it in the coals when I had some. My menu would consist of hors d'oeuvres of Witchetty Grubs, (these I had brought with me, still in the wood; twenty of them, purchased from a contact in Alice Springs for $3 each). Kangaroo Tail Soup, Puftaloons, and a main course that I'd called Chicken Wokup, to be served with the damper. Lastly, I had prepared a sweets course of Quandongs with cream (Quandongs are Australian native peaches and a friend of mine called Brian Powell, from the Flinders Ranges, had kindly supplied these out-of-season Quandongs). This serve of Quandong sweets was in the form of a slice, and needed to be reconstituted by heating.

It was now around midday, getting hotter all the time, and I was sitting with my back against my swag, reading a book, as I had done all I could do as far as the meal was concerned. Apart from the muted city noises in the background, I could have easily been in the bush, but a couple of incidents that were about to occur, soon reinforced the fact that I wasn't.

From under my hat, I noticed a lady, with a small dog on a lead, coming along a walking track towards me. I briefly visualised what confronted her. She would see a fire, surrounded by my camp, with most of the objects probably unidentifiable. She would then focus on a bloke in bush gear, leaning against a swag. The marked pause in her progress would have been when she noticed the rifle, also leaning against the swag. From that moment on, her body language portrayed deep agitation, but still she continued towards me, the fluffy little toy dog uttering a sharp yelp. When she was almost opposite me, and some ten metres away, I called out, "How are you going?" I never found out, because no sooner were the words out of my mouth, when she bloody near throttled the ball of fluff on the lead, as her legs went into speed walking mode. A badly rattled citizen I thought, and wondered how on earth I stacked up in her thought processes.

Whilst the situation did provide a welcome contrast to my somewhat boring book, I wasn't aware of the negative aspects. One phone call to the boys in blue, and the day's format might have seen some radical changes.

I didn't have long to dwell upon this, as another walker appeared on the track. I must admit that I was beginning to enjoy this situation. From under my hat, once again, I summed up this new player on the block. I classified him, in modern day terminology, as a househusband. Well turned out in sporty shorts, with a t-shirt saying 'JUST DO IT', and a pair of expensive-looking Reeboks or similar. Attached to him on a lead was an up-market looking Dalmatian, which probably hadn't bailed up a lot of rats in its life.

A confident (up until this moment) Sydney-sider in his early thirties, who probably had a professional partner, earning heaps more than he did. Hence his househusband status – well that was my interpretation.

As I secretly observed him, surveying the scene before him, his confidence started to ebb. He was confronted by a bloke, lounging on his swag with his rifle at his elbow, surrounded by a heap of weird looking gear; plus a large fire on a hot summer's day, and not a vehicle in sight. If his brain had become a bit under-worked of late, then it suddenly had a big rev-up today. Before he'd finalised his escape plan, I looked up and hit him with a "Howaya goin mate? Orright?" He replied with some unidentifiable nervous response. I noticed that he'd slowed right down to the slowest possible gait, but still kept moving. He wasn't going to get caught flat-footed.

The ensuing conversation went something like this. "This is a bit of a mongrel camp" I said "No feed anywhere." He just gawked and kept on slowly moving. I continued, "Yeah, I've just come south looking for work. My camels are down by that big salt waterhole trying to get a feed." The househusband kept moving, almost imperceptibly, a wild look appearing in his eyes. "Who owns the pub in Sydney?" I demanded, and with a desperate, almost incoherent, "I don't know." He also engaged full throttle in the speed walking mode. I noticed that the classy Dalmatian had handled this sudden acceleration a lot better than had the ball of fluff.

I kept thinking about phone calls to the Police, reporting a 'weirdo' in Castlecrag Park, or wherever I was, but I reasoned that it probably wouldn't happen. These days people don't like to get involved, not a good thing, but in my favour on this occasion.

Soon afterwards, a 4-wheel drive vehicle arrived, towing a trailer with a camel aboard. It was Stafford Bullen of Bullen's Circus, who unloaded a very nice little female camel called Sugar Lips, and put a riding saddle on her. Stafford explained that this camel didn't like to hoosh down, so he had to take a people-loading ramp out of the trailer. This is a good idea when a camel has to give consistent short rides, saving the constant getting up and down.

Stafford left, and soon after, the Centre Point people arrived, unloading a massive cauldron of buffalo stew, put together by the head chef. A coach closely followed this, with the media contingent aboard. From then on, it was fast and furious. I gave rides for about half an hour, trying to extol the virtues of a 40-Day camel expedition to a hyped-up journo, reluctantly doing a 3-minute ride. In between times, I still had to tend my cooking department, so I finally tied up Sugar Lips, secretly thinking that she could be better employed to the west of the Blue Mountains.

I then began cooking my well-travelled Witchetties on a shovel. A lady journalist, in her mid twenties, came up to me and identified herself as a representative of AAP Reuters, the overseas news service. She had me worried from the start with her first question, as the grubs curled up on the hot shovel. She asked, "Don't you think that's a cruel way to cook those grubs?" This wasn't the sort of question I was looking for; I mean there's not a lot of ways you can cook a Witchetty Grub. So, with a confidence that I didn't really feel, I said, "They don't feel a thing." to which the journalist lady replied, "Oh! Are you a medical person?" Now this was starting to put me off my game, and I had to try to keep my cool, not an easy task, hanging over one of the hottest cooking fires on earth. I told her that, although I wasn't a medical person, I just knew that the grubs died an instant death, the moment they contacted the hot shovel. All this time she was writing furiously, and I had visions of being internationally roasted, worse than any Witchetty Grub ever had been. (In fact, her article turned out to be as positive as any, and I could hardly believe it).

In between courses, I told a few tales of the bush and the tucker seemed to be going down OK. The party would alternate between my camp and the Centre Point setup. A columnist from one of the Sydney Dailies took a great interest in my Quandong dessert. Turns out he was born in Leonora, in Western Australia's eastern goldfields, where Quandongs are widespread. Said he hadn't tasted a Quandong since he was a kid, so he was tickled pink (red) with the serve.

About mid afternoon, the coach pulled out with the journalists, and I thought that I had received some good mileage; hard yakka for a few hours, but quite enjoyable, nonetheless. Sugar Lips was collected as my plant was, once again, stacked in and on the Holden. As we were leaving, a Government car pulled up, disgorging a couple of suits armed with clipboards, so I couldn't help thinking that this may have involved some of the publicity that I wasn't looking for.

I'm not sure who won the cooking competition, but it didn't seem to matter. Back then to the airport for my cargo and myself, for the flight back to Adelaide. I had arranged with the cargo department to collect my camp the following day, so I headed for the luggage carousel to collect a personal bag. As I approached, I noticed that there appeared to be some amusement rippling through the crowd of business types. Looking over towards the carousel, I noticed this object struggling to get out, an object that I soon recognised to be the back end of my packsaddle. Those cargo blokes, I felt sure, were playing a little game. Eventually the saddle was spat out, causing a murmur of amused laughter. This saddle was closely followed by my posthole shovel, a single roll of toilet paper and my rifle. At this moment,

I thought it would be a good time to make a departure. As I left I noticed a still stuffed pack bag, trying to get through an opening three quarters its size. I laughingly abused the cargo department, and told them that I'd be back to collect it the next day. If it really is Sydney or the bush, I'll take the bush every time.

15.

The 44 of Port

I had to pick up a group from Quilpie in southwest Queensland, which meant a three-day drive from McLaren Flat. Bill Oliver and Fred Osmond were the drivers, and we set off in three vehicles, me driving a D131, 4x4 International, with Fred and Bill both driving Land Rover station wagons. We very much enjoyed these 'dry runs' to pick up parties, and this one proved to be one of the most eventful. The first night we camped in the Strzelecki creek, about thirty kilometres south of Merty Merty homestead. We pulled up late in the afternoon, and soon had the swags out and occupied.

Next morning, after a leisurely breakfast, we headed up the track, calling in at Merty homestead. A semi trailer was pulled up on the flat, and we noticed that there were three blokes sitting under the trailer. We walked across and said "G'day." After the usual exchanges, I asked the Merty blokes, Teddy Reich the owner, Brian Arrowsmith and another bloke, if they would like a port. It was eight o'clock in the morning, and in this part of the world, it was not an unusual question. They answered in the affirmative, so I went back to my truck, and dug out a flagon of Southern Vales Port. We blokes got our pannikins, and moved under the trailer with the Merty blokes. What followed was a minor session that lasted for a couple of hours, until the flagon was drained. A lot of stories were told, and subjects discussed, and just before we departed, Teddy asked "Rex! Where could a man get some more of this?" I told him that it could easily be arranged, and asked him, half seriously, if he required half a dozen 'goons', or a 44. A faraway look came into Teddy's eyes as he asked, "Is that really possible?" I told him that it certainly was, so he placed a very firm order. I said that I would organize it as soon as I returned home. Now many promises are made over part-empty flagons of port, most of them never being kept, but I have always tried to be a man of my word, and made myself an indelible mental note.

We headed off up the deserted Strzelecki Track, sure in the knowledge that nasties like breathalysers had yet to be invented. We also knew that breathalyser operators were pretty thin on the ground in these parts as well. Author's note: Things do change though as, only in1997, we were driving my OKA out to Coongie Lakes near Innamincka. Ben Crabb, from Kangaroo Island, was driving, and as we came around a bend, there on the track was a Police Land Rover. They pulled us up and they asked Crabby to blow in the bag; so you never know. (The Innamincka races were taking part a kilometre or two down the track).

We took two days to get over to Quilpie, and quite memorable days they were too. In my book, *Mulga Madness*, I've already described our encounter with this car thief at the Nuccundra pub, so will not dwell on it here. However, I will relate an interesting incident that happened, the night after our little session under the semi trailer. We were camped in Sturt Stoney Desert country, on Naryilco station, and Fred brought out two bottles of unlabelled dry red, with which we started to wash down some grilled steak. The steak came from my cousins, John and Jill Ellis, whose meat is always top class, and comes from their McLaren Vale butcher shop. The red wine was from Scarpantoni winery at McLaren Flat. Don Scarpantoni would pick some of his best grapes each year, making top class wine for his family, and quite often, he would give Fred some of these. It was of 'Blood Bank' quality, so we were thoroughly enjoying it. Although I make mention of the wine's quality, I really don't think it had any bearing on what happened next.

We were well into the second bottle, when we noticed something above, some breakaway country silhouetted against the sky in the north. A green and red light was moving along, parallel with the top of the level breakaway or tableland, seeming to be about two hundred feet above it, moving slowly along; It completely held our attention. There was absolutely no logical explanation for what we were seeing, and after about four or five seconds, the two lights, one above the other, suddenly went straight up, for what seemed like a hundred metres, then continued on in a parallel line. After perhaps six seconds, they again went upward, and then ran parallel again for several seconds, before disappearing. The whole event lasted no more than a half a minute, so we spent the rest of the evening discussing it, eventually putting it down as a U.F.O. I have seen a lot of unusual phenomena during my outback travels, but this was the most distinctive. Next morning there was only a couple of fork-tailed kites, circling lazily where the action had been, the whole events of the previous night seemed like a dream. However, we were all positive about what we had seen. We eventually arrived in Quilpie, picked up the party, and operated a very worthwhile trip, back on the Cooper.

When I returned home, I went to see the Manager of Southern Vales Winery, (now known as Tattachilla Wines) and I asked Bill Slattery if he would mind sending a 44 of port up to Merty Station. I guaranteed the payment, and Bill very much appreciated the order; I think more the circumstances than the actual sale. After that, I forgot all about it, being out of that general area for some time.

It was almost two years later that I was heading up the bore track from Cameron Corner, when I called into Bollards Lagoon, a large cattle station, located in the eastern side of the Strzelecki Desert. At the time, Bollards Lagoon was owned by George Reich, Ted's brother. It adjoined Merty Merty, and both of the brothers worked together a fair bit. As I drove into the homestead area, it appeared that the station was deserted, no vehicles around, and an air of inactivity. I pulled up, telling my passengers to stay in the vehicle, and wandered over to the homestead. As I approached the building, the door opened, and out come a barrel of a man under a huge 10-gallon bush hat. I recognized the jovial face of Ross Scobie, an old Birdsville Track identity, and one of the great bush yarn spinners. I have heard him spin yarn after yarn, all supposedly true, for hours on end, a real natural. Well, on this occasion, Ross told a very interesting story, one in which I was very much involved.

It appeared that nearly two years ago, he was caretaking Bollards Lagoon, just as he was on this occasion. It was mail day; a time eagerly anticipated on all outback runs, usually occurring once a week. The Tibooburra mail truck pulled into the station yard, and the driver and Ross began to unload a variety of items, apart from the mailbag. One of these items was a blue 44-gallon drum that he looked at with some intensity. Ross went on, "Rex! I'd never seen a drum like it. It had a full size, crimped lid (no bung) and she was a 'cleanskin', so I rolled it off under the verandah. After a while, the mail truck left and I boiled the billy to make a cuppa tea. I sat there staring at that drum, trying to work out what was in it. It couldn't have been petrol or diesel and it wasn't oil of any kind; I'd never seen a drum with a top like that. I tried to sleep that night, Rex, but that blue 44 kept coming up in my mind.

"After breakfast next morning, I couldn't stand the pressure any longer, and I decided to open the bastard. It took a while, but I eventually got the lid released; there was a smell that was half familiar to me. I lifted it off Rex, and I thought I was having the 'horrors'! I thought it was a cruel joke, mate. I was staring at a 44 of plonk! Forty-four gallons of it.

"I didn't do anything for a minute, I had to go and sit down for a bit. I've had a bit of good fortune in my life, and this looked like some more to me; but it could be a nasty trick, I'd had a few played on me in my time. After a minute or two, I went into the kitchen and got a pannikin, and I walked up to the drum and dipped it in. I took a sip and a great feeling of well-being came over me. Rex! It was port, mate.

"Well, I finished the pannikin, put the lid back on, and wheeled the drum over to the corner of the yard. Both Bollards Lagoon and Merty are built on sandhills, with a corrugated iron fence surrounding the homestead and shedding, keeping the drift sand at bay in dry times. I built a timber frame around the 44, with a bit of a spinifex thatching to keep the sun off. After that, I settled down to see what would happen. I rationed myself to a 'certain number' of pannikins a day and life really looked up.

"But it also changed because, prior to the port, I wouldn't see a soul in weeks, but a few days after it arrived, I got the first visitor. I saw the dust, and eventually a Toyota rolled up. A bloke who I vaguely remembered got out, and came up and said G'Day. Rex, he couldn't look me in the eyes, he talked about the weather, and nothing in particular, but his eyes kept sliding off toward the drum of port. In the end, I offered him a pannikin, and he couldn't accept it quick enough.

"Now the mystery is, how the bloody hell did the word get around? I didn't have a vested interest in spreading it, did I? It's just one of those mysteries; never did trust the crows around here. Anyway, to cut a long story short, I saw blokes I hadn't seen in years, and in a couple of months the drum was drained."

When I was talking to Ted Reich, some months later, he told me that the drum had a wide-ranging effect on the country. There were several near divorces, along with other varied dramas. He really appreciated me keeping my word, but thought that perhaps they wouldn't order another drum; not for a while, anyway.

16.

A Cameleer in India

For a number of years we had a general sales agent in Sydney called Ausventure, owned and operated by Warwick Deacock. They organised adventure holidays all around the world, and I had been asked to lead a trip to India and Nepal. My wife, Patti, was to accompany me and our party consisted of twelve people, some of whom were old clients of mine.

It was a very exciting, incident-filled couple of weeks, starting even before we left the Land of Oz. We were sitting in the Air India Jumbo at the Perth airport when we noticed a mobile ladder, racing out towards the plane. It was erected next to one of the engines, a panel was opened up, and someone started tapping at its innards. I asked one of the Indian flight stewards if there was any trouble, to which she replied in a rather irritated manner, "There is nothing wrong", before sweeping off down the aisle, nearly smothering me in her sari; real good for the confidence.

Our flight to New Delhi was, however, quite uneventful, and we plunged into the sights, sounds and smells of the sub-continent. It was November and the weather was hot, but not unbearably so. Our job was to act like a mother hen to the party, and in the airport, we had a very efficient and pleasant Indian called Nandi, resplendent in a dark blue "bag of fruit", who was to help get us through the unbelievable bureaucracy of the airport administration. Nandi represented I.T.A. the Indian travel organisation.

Boarding a flotilla of three-wheeled taxis, we set out through a sea of humanity for our hotel. I started to feel a little bit claustrophobic but thought, 'I'm going to have to get used to this." We duly arrived at our accommodation, which truly was a luxury hotel, complete with a glass, see-through lift, up one side of the multi-storey building. I very soon realised that India was a land of contradictions, because when I turned on the hot water tap in our excellent accommodation, a cockroach came out, followed by no hot water; or any water for that matter. Still I wasn't complaining, it added a bit of character to the place.

Our schedule included a couple of days in New Delhi, before taking a train to Rajasthan to do a three-day camel trek, on the edge of the Thar Desert, then it was back to New Delhi for a day or two before flying to Nepal. We had a couple of days just wandering around New Delhi, and one incident that springs to mind is one that I'll never forget.

There were plenty of "floor shows" wherever we went in the streets, with lots of fangless Cobras rising up out of baskets, to the tune of their handlers. Beggars were ever present, and one soon learnt to develop a thick skin where they were concerned. It's like killing a fly; if you swat one, a thousand others come to its funeral, and the beggars were just like that. We came across something special, where a bloke was sitting in the gutter, playing some sort of flute-like instrument. He had with him two monkeys on chains, one with a small set of bongo drums, and the other, presumably a female, resplendent in a pink ballerina dress. I thought this couldn't be fair dinkum until the man began to play a fast tune with plenty of rhythm. Immediately, the bongo drummer began to play, the ballerina began to dance, and what really was amazing was the fact that they were both in time with the music. I play bongo drums myself and I think that monkey could have left me for dead. The performance only lasted for a couple of minutes, and when they had finished, a few of us clapped and we all put money into his bowl. All, that is, but for one member of our party who was a bit tight with his money. As we went to walk away, the Indian said something, and the little female monkey sprang off his lap, and when she reached the end of her chain, snapped at our member's leg, missing it by inches. We then told our miserable mate what we thought of him, and made him put in double. It was an incredible bit of animal training and I only hoped that the monkeys were well looked after.

On the evening of the second day in New Delhi, we had to catch a train down to Rajasthan, so we booked out of the pub and headed for the railway station in taxis. Nandi was with us to help get us loaded onto the train, and as we entered the platform area of the station, yet another spectacle presented itself. We couldn't see the platform for people, most sitting or lying down, and Nandi explained to us that this was home for many of them, whilst others were just camped there, waiting for trains. We walked around and stepped over this mass of humanity, whilst our porters tagged along behind, carrying our gear.

After a good twenty minutes or so we arrived, supposedly at our destination. Shortly afterwards a train appeared out of the gloom that was wood smoke and other pollutants in the air. However, something was wrong. Between our platform and another across the way were two sets of tracks, and the train was approaching on the far set. I glanced at Nandi and saw that all the colour seemed to be sliding downward in his face, like when you pulled the lever on one of those old-fashioned petrol bowsers to dump the contents. He stood there, as white as it was possible for an Indian to look. He said to me "Mr Rex, This is very terrible" and started wringing his hands. I could see the problem all right, this was our train but we were on the wrong platform.

When the train came to a standstill, all the garbage and the food scraps from the kitchen carriage were thrown onto the adjacent tracks. In the gloom, I could see these large animal shapes, bobbing around everywhere. It was as though about twenty wheat bags full of Ringtail Possums had been released, but I soon realised that these shapes were in fact, huge numbers of rats, the largest that I had ever seen.

The end of the train had pulled up almost past our position, so I said to Nandi. "Why don't we just hop down onto the tracks and walk over to the other platform?" This seemed to upset him even more as he replied "Mr Rex, it is not possible. It's the rat, the rats, besides it's illegal." I said to him "These Australians are funny buggers. Just hang on a minute and I'll have a yarn to them." I explained to the party, a fair bit of what they already knew, we were here and our train was over there. I noticed that they couldn't take their eyes off the rats, so I told them I had a proposition to put to them, and I got their attention. I must mention here that not every member of this party was what you might describe as adventure travel material. Some of them were well past their physical best, and probably their mental best as well. I was very aware that they had put their trust fully in me, so what I was about to suggest to them, couldn't be found in the trip description notes of any brochure. I was aware of all that, and I was also aware of the fact that I had a mob of Australians, and that I'd probably get away with it.

"Here's what we have to do," I told them "we have to hop off this platform, walk across the tracks, and hop up onto the other platform." I have long realised that when you give people unpalatable information, it's never wise to look them in the eye, just watch their Adam's apple. Many of these, I noticed, were doing loop the loops in their throats, indicating a sense of great anxiety. I also noticed that some of the members seemed to welcome this development. Taking their silence to indicate in the affirmative, I went back to Nandi with the good news. He was dying a thousand deaths, aware that there would be a line of people stretching from here to the Taj Mahal queuing to take his job.

I told him that the job was on, and he stared at me unbelievably, so I left him and went about organising the crossing. There were two old clients of mine who concerned me a little, one of whom was Russell, an old war correspondent. He was always dressed immaculately in a blue suit with brilliantly polished, very expensive black shoes. Russell was in his seventies, and always had a very caustic wit, but he was by no means the healthiest member of our party. His wife Eve was a tiny little lady, and I thought, only half jokingly, that were she to fall over, a rat might well carry her off. Anyway, I decided that it would be best if I was to piggyback her across the tracks, and she also thought that was a good idea. Everyone, including Nandi, was ready for the crossing, though he did have a sort of glazed look in his eyes.

We jumped down onto the tracks, and an amazing thing happened. The hubbub of people noise suddenly stopped, and you could almost hear a crowbar drop. We didn't dare to look, but we could feel that thousands of pairs of eyes were fixed upon us. Stepping carefully, we began to cover the twenty metres or so to the other platform. All around our feet, the huge rats scurried, and I'm pretty sure it wouldn't have been a very good idea to fall over; they showed no fear of us. We were almost across when Russell uttered an oath. He raised one of his previously immaculate shoes onto the platform, in front of a very fine looking old man, dressed in ragged clothing, but with a nice looking white turban. "Look at what this bastard Ellis has made me do!" exploded Russell. His expensive shoe was covered in rat guts, from a dead one that he had obviously stepped on. We all hopped up onto the platform, and as suddenly as it had stopped, the noise started up again, with nobody taking much notice of us. Nandi was gradually regaining some of his natural colour, and he was beginning to smile, with an incredible respect for Australians.

We boarded our train and travelled through the night; aware of the fact that there were probably as many people camped on the roof, as there were inside the carriages. In the daylight, we could see the desert lands of Rajasthan, with the odd settlement here and there. On arrival at the town of Jaisalmer, we were taken through streets full of all sorts of wheeled traffic, but I also noticed the large number of camels, mostly towing camel carts. Also very noticeable was the excellent condition of all the camels that I had seen in India. That night we spent in a hotel that was a converted Maharaja's palace, a huge sprawling building with massive rooms. We slept in one of these rooms that had colourfully decorated walls and ceiling, no problems with claustrophobia in this place.

Next morning, after a sumptuous breakfast, a mini bus came to pick us up. It was to take us to a village on the edge of the Thar Desert, where we would start our three-day camel trek, the first such tourist trek to be organised in this area. I had been doing a bit of reading, and had found out about a rat temple that contained a sect of rat worshippers, somewhere in the area, that might make an interesting diversion; would surely provide a bit of contrast to those other big blokes, scurrying around at the railway station two days ago.

We loaded up our gear, and I had a yarn to our driver about this little diversion, plus another one that I had in mind. Now there are drivers and there are drivers, and we decided that this one should have been doing something else for a crust. He didn't like people and he didn't like us in particular, especially when I mentioned the rat temple; said it wasn't on the itinerary. I told him that it was new to the area and that we wanted to see it, after all, the vehicle was at my disposal, and we had ample time. He argued about it, but it didn't do him any good, so we started off with a gear change that the gearbox would remember for the rest of its life.

After an hour, we turned off the main road and drove for another twenty minutes to our destination. As we emerged from a patch of very thorny bush,

On the Wrong Side of the Tracks

we came across a modern, single storey temple. There were several Indians, clad in white, who all seemed most surprised by our visit. (This temple is now a well-visited tourist attraction). A very imposing gentleman came over to welcome us, so I explained our interest. He was genuinely pleased, and he took us inside to a type of courtyard, where we were confronted by an amazing spectacle; hundreds of rats occupied the place. They were across the well-swept dirt yard; sitting on tables and benches, and some were lying around, asleep. Others were feeding on grain and milk, their staple diet, and all were fat and shiny, and they looked one in the eye. These had to be the most respectable members of *Ratus Ratus* anywhere on earth.

Then occurred an incident that sort of blotted our copybook, involving a lively English couple called Lance and Pat. Now Lance was a good man with a video camera, and as he stood there capturing the scenes before him, a large, sleek rat ran up Pat's leg, up her back and sat upon her head; happened as quick as you can say Ratsak. Lance, always the professional, trained the camera on his wife and kept on shooting, capturing the whole event on tape. Pat froze, and fixing Lance with a steely gaze, ordered him to stop his videoing. Lance didn't stop; well not immediately, and I'm sure he must have paid for this indiscretion later on, as erring husbands sometimes can. The head ratcatcher was summoned to remove the rat, but the beast had no intention of letting go. The rat man took hold of it, and Pat gave a bit of a squawk as it dug its claws into her scalp. Lance got the video camera going again, and the thought went through my mind that there was one very brave man. The rat man pulled harder, and eventually the rat let go, only to reattach itself to his finger, nearly biting through it, as blood went everywhere. It soon released its grip and ran back down onto the ground, obviously deciding that that this was definitely the time to depart. Lance and Pat seemed to be having a heated, though whispered, conversation, but we were all pleased to have had such an amusing floorshow.

An hour later, we had our second diversion, which was to a Government camel farm that I had heard about, a relatively new initiative. We pulled up in front of these immaculate brick buildings, and went inside for a look. It was as though someone had dropped a neutron bomb, there was not a soul to be seen. Plenty of excellent camels, many of them bulls, were inside this compound, and I can't remember having seen finer looking beasts. I was sorry that there was nobody around to tell us about them, as it would have been very interesting to hear what was going on. Camels are most important animals in India, because apart from ordinary uses, the army uses them to patrol the Rajasthan – Pakistan border, a unit called the Indian Camel Corps.

We drove on from there and considered looking for a spot to have our lunch; I couldn't rely on our driver to do anything more than drive the bus which, fortunately, he did quite well. In the distance, I could see some people working in a paddock full of maize. There was a huge mound of grain, with about half a dozen Indian women standing around, threshing it with beating sticks; they looked a bit like those plastic leaf rakes. I asked the driver to stop, but he didn't want to so, but when he saw that I was becoming a bit annoyed, he reluctantly brought the bus to a halt, and withdrew into his seat, sulking. I told everyone in the bus that this was to be our lunch break, so they all hopped out and prepared themselves for their midday meal.

I wasn't going to let an Indian experience like this go to waste, so I started to walk over towards the workers. Suddenly I saw that the male in charge of the group had started to walk rapidly towards me, yelling and waving his arms in an excited fashion. I kept on smiling and called out to him, "How are you going, mate? All right?" as he stormed up to me. I saw that he was a fine looking desert man, but I could also see that he wasn't at all happy. He ignored my greeting, continuing with his abuse, but I just kept on smiling, and invited them all to join us for lunch. As my people walked closer, he slowed down a little, so I offered him a cheese and lettuce roll; that stopped him altogether. In another ten minutes, the whole scenario had changed drastically. Our girls were all having a go at threshing the maize, while the Rajasthan women were all sitting around, smiling and laughing and enjoying a big lunch. The boss man wasn't laughing, although he wasn't having such a bad time either. The fact that none of us could converse, made little difference to our enjoyment, and it was with some reluctance that we finally drifted back to our mini bus with its disgruntled driver. One of our girls, Cathy, suggested that perhaps we could try thrashing him with one of the maize threshing sticks.

We travelled on until we finally arrived at a small village on the edge of the Thar Desert, where we were shown some tent accommodation. The people here were very impressive, living a desert existence, with few concessions to western civilization. We wandered around and listened to a Sitar playing, that melancholy stringed instrument that seemed well suited to this situation. The people showed much curiosity towards us, not having seen many westerners, but were never rude about it.

Just on dusk, our Wallahs, mounted on large bull camels, began to make their appearance. This was a very impressive sight, one that will remain in my memory for a very long time to come. The lowering sun in the western sky, bathed the desert dunes in a surreal rosy glow. Any sunsets in this part of the world had to penetrate the wood smoke pollution, even though it was not so apparent as it is in the cities. The camels appeared individually and in pairs, from all points of the compass. There were fourteen of them, and they had been contracted from various villages for this first-time trek.

We went over to the group and introduced ourselves, and as I had brought with me fourteen photographs of my camels, I presented one of these to each of the Wallahs. They seemed to be very impressed with this, and they viewed me with new respect. By their reasoning, anyone who owned twenty five camels, must be the Aussie equivalent of an Indian Maharaja, or better. Soon after, what turned out to be the head Wallah approached me and indicated that he wished me to ride with him tomorrow. None of them could speak fluent English, although some did have a few words, a bit like our command of their language.

Soon after dawn next day, we assembled at the staging area where there were camels hooshed down all over the place. There were several camels towing large, two-wheeled carts that would carry our gear. These carts, I observed, were fitted with aircraft tyres, an interesting blend of the ancient and the modern. I was also interested to note just how Spartan the camels' saddles were. The front parts, where the riders were to sit, consisted of half-round timber, with no padding to speak of, and the stirrups were lengths of binder twine. I didn't much like the look of this, as many of my people had never ridden *any* animal before. The whole trek was to be in the charge of a picture theatre owner, and the more I saw of him, the less I liked him. He was a real smart arse, riding around on a fine-looking, almost pure black, bull. My concerns were falling on deaf ears, but I did manage to get Russ a berth in one of the camel carts, where he looked pretty comfortable, reading a book, under an umbrella.

Eventually we all got aboard, but I was a bit worried about my lack of involvement, and I could see that many safety factors had been neglected. However, all of a sudden, the camels jumped up and we were away at the jog. Now I'm well used to riding camels, but these saddles were not good, so I knew then that some of the party were going to get very sore. My Wallah was in charge, so he made his way to the front of the mob. As we passed various others, I was interested to note that many of the Wallahs had their arms around the waists of the female passengers, whose faces registered anything from wild alarm, to stark terror. I was powerless however, to do a bloody thing about it, so I just had to go with the flow. Our English-speaking, picture theatre owner, head camel man was by this time, little more than a cloud of dust in the distance.

Things sort of settled down, as much as they were going to, so I started to enjoy the experience. My Wallah was smoking an evil-looking, thin, foul-smelling cigarette, and every now and then, he would offer me a puff, but I kept declining. We travelled single file through several villages, and we were very impressed by just how immaculate they were; no sign of western rubbish, like fast food wrappers or cool drink cans. Often we even saw women sweeping the dirt in front of their houses.

There were numerous stages of the camels' staple diet, the dry, prickly vegetation of the dominant Acacia tree. Most of the trees are pruned, or stripped of their foliage and this is stored, later to be fed to the animals like hay. It must be full of protein and nutrition, evidenced by the condition of the local camels. That night we made camp on the outskirts of another village. We were actually travelling a route around the edge of the Thar Desert, passing grazing animals and sparse crops. Many of our people were bandy-legged and sore around the camp that night, so a couple of us managed to gather some rags and cloths for a bit of extra padding, hopefully to improve the saddles somewhat. Wooden tables and chairs were set up, with white linen tablecloths. There was heavy china crockery and stainless steel cutlery, so the whole thing reminded me of something out of Doctor Livingstone. The meals were good and there was plenty to go round. The curries were pretty rugged so we washed them down with huge jugs of water and Indian beer. During the evening, I tried to find the picture theatre manager, to try to have a serious discussion with him; but he had vanished.

At about midday next day, an interesting incident occurred. We had entered a larger than usual village, and had hooshed down somewhere in the middle. Nearby was a well, surrounded by large, shady trees, a very pleasant spot. No sooner had we dismounted, than along came three Indian Scoutmasters, complete with toggles and knobbly knees. They homed in on me, shaking my hand (left one) vigorously, with much welcoming. This was all very perplexing, but I decided to go along with it, to see what might happen. We were all invited to have a meal with them, but we decided that we should just have tea, wary of the local tucker for fear of tummy wogs. We all crowded into a large tent for a time of confused conversation. It soon dawned on me that I had been mistaken for the main man, the local Baden Powell. It appeared that they were having some sort of a jamboree and were expecting the top brass to inspect the proceedings. Now I realise that the wise and proper thing to do would be to fold our tents, as it were, and disappear into the distance, but unfortunately, it's not in my nature to do something like that. Here was an opportunity that I simply couldn't resist.

They led the way, my party following like an entourage, not knowing just what to expect. We soon came across three rows of tents, maybe a hundred or so, swarming with Scouts, who looked at me with something resembling awe, so I realised that I was in this situation for the long haul. It became immediately obvious that I was expected to carry out an inspection of the ranks, so that's exactly what I did. I patted heads here, tightened toggles there, adjusted some of their knots and went through all the motions. I may have been an impostor, but everyone seemed to be having a good time. Patti kept hissing in my ear that it was time to get out of there, but I was having too much fun for that. We finally arrived at the last tent and we were led down to a parade ground, where poles flew Indian and British flags.

It was here that one of the Scoutmasters conveyed to me that I was to impose some sort of blessing on the group. I thought that this was where I was going to come unstuck, and I began to sweat a bit. I decided that perhaps I should have a crack at the Lord's Prayer, hoping that this might do the trick. All the Scouts were lined up on a slight rise, about thirty metres in front of us. After I had finished the blessing, they all gave a loud war cry, raised their staffs and started to rush towards us. The very first thing that raced through my mind was that we were going to be killed with sticks, on a Rajasthan playing field. The three hundred or so boys however, suddenly came to a halt several metres from us, and started to applaud, much to my relief. I could see that most of my mob too, had been taken in by the performance. By now I reckoned that it was definitely time to take our leave, so bidding our goodbyes, we hurried back to the camels. Not bothering too much about a sedentary lunch, we headed out of town. I often wonder what happened when the genuine article arrived back there. Maybe he was killed with the sticks.

That night we camped near another village, where I eventually managed to round up the picture theatre man. I explained to him some of my concerns, quite politely, but he pretended that he didn't understand what I was saying; though I knew full well that he did. I persevered for a while, but to no avail, until eventually I did my block, calling him a number of things; but it all seemed like water off a duck's back. Finally, in a state of total frustration, I yelled at him, "You're nothing but a little shit." Well! You wouldn't believe the change that came over him. All of a sudden, he was full of concern, and immediately paid attention to my requests. I was dumfounded, amazed at the complete change in the man. We sat down together then and proceeded to iron out some of the problems, such as the camels strung out over a couple of kilometres, and me not being in touch with him. Wonders will never cease; perhaps the word, shit, has a lot of relevance in India, but I really didn't know. I was just so pleased that it had worked in his case.

After lunch the next day, we approached the sacred town of Pushkar, consisting of a huge Palace/Fort, next to a lake, with the township scattered around it. As we reached the outskirts, we passed hundreds of animals, and people with camps everywhere. Most of the animals were camels, with a smattering of donkeys and ponies, with just a few cattle. This, we were told, was the annual Pushkar camel fair, and the sand dunes surrounding the town, were literally black with camels, ten thousand of them, according to one of the men. The main object of the fair was for the calves to be sold off to the buyers, who with the sellers, came from far and wide throughout the country. This really was a most impressive spectacle, to me and to my group. The Indians like bright colours, and here there was colour for as far as the eye could see. Reds, greens and blues were everywhere, all brightly clothed, even down to some colourful tattoos on many of the camels.

We were taken to what was described as a tent hotel, which consisted of about a hundred tents, all joined together, and heading away over a couple of sand dunes like a great long snake. We were each shown a tent, and we settled in for what was going to be a two-night stay. As the sun sank behind the dunes, the whole area became a hotbed of activity. There were musicians scattered everywhere, with all sorts of street theatre pulsating away in the hot night. Some of us walked down to the lake, partly covered with beautiful water lilies, but the main feature was the presence of the huge sacred fish. The local women used to have a ritual of swimming nude with the fish, a custom that had recently been discontinued; due largely to the increase in the numbers of perverts visiting the region. These large fish rose to the surface of the water, taking food from the hands of the dozens of local people. Apart from finding a scorpion in our "hotel" room, we all had a good night's sleep, the bedding being a bit more substantial than our cigarette paper mattresses that we were using on the camel trek.

A fair bit of the time next day, was spent riding around with our Wallahs, inspecting all the varied activities. There were all sorts of bartering and dealing going on, between the buyers and the sellers, as well as constant pony racing. The numbers of camels in the whole area was simply mind blowing. Up until now, I had only ever seen about three hundred in a single group. I also couldn't help but notice the very large number of black camels. The Australian animals are descendants of the sub-continent camels, but it is pretty near impossible to find an entirely black beast. At one stage I asked my Wallah if I could try on his huge turban, a request that I regretted, as I finished up with it, and he with my hat. I was amazed at its weight, but it was composed of about ten metres of cloth. It finally ended up as curtains in our daughters' bedrooms.

After a memorable three days, we bade farewell to our camel men, boarded a mini bus, and headed for the train. It was an interesting trip, back to another classy hotel in New Delhi, a stark contrast to our tent hotel on the Sandhill. We spent a couple of days here, looking at the Red Fort etc., plus we took a day trip down to Agra to see the famous Taj Mahal. Travelling on Indian roads leaves one with a sense of amazement; amazing that one has survived the day of total chaos. In the event of a road traffic accident, the participants simply bolt. They run away for fear of being beaten to death on the spot, by angry relatives or passers by. Another eyebrow raiser was the number of Indian men, defecating on the median strips and the roadsides. I could, however, see no sign of previous such activity, a fact that occupied my thoughts for a while thereafter. Some time later, I found that the answer to this question was pigs. Apparently, they move in at night and clean the whole show up; says a lot for being a vegetarian. The Taj Mahal has been well documented, so I won't dwell on it here, though it certainly is one the great man-made wonders of the world, well worth a visit.

The following day, we all flew north to Nepal, an interesting and spectacular flight, particularly the descent into Kathmandu, through the Himalayan Mountains. The first thing that we noticed, on leaving the plane, was the transformation from the Indian heat, to the Nepalese climate. We had a very interesting five days in this tiny country, which included a three-day river raft trip, from the Himalayan foothills to the Chitwan National Park on the plains. Here we had a night in tent accommodation, plus a night in Tiger Tops, a massive tree house. The night before this, we were hurriedly taken from our tents, through a sort of tunnel affair, and into a jungle hide. A young buffalo had been slaughtered, and had been laid out as a lure for tigers. We were told that one was in the vicinity tonight, so we all hoped to get a look at it. When the floodlights were put on briefly, we had a momentary glimpse of a large tiger at the kill, for which we all considered ourselves very fortunate.

The main activity at Tiger Tops, was a two-hour elephant safari, searching for tigers. We stepped straight off a loading bay, attached to the viewing platform of Tiger Tops, onto the riding platform on the back of the elephant. There were four of us on this ride, each in a corner of the platform, hanging on to the rail, with our legs dangling either side of the corner posts. We headed off, part of a line of about half a dozen animals, through open forests and grasslands. The grass was quite tall, often almost half the height of the elephants. I must say that the view from the back of an elephant is much better than that from a camel, but that's where it ended. The elephant handler, or Mahout, had the best position, sitting directly behind the ears, where there was very little movement of the body. He gained his position by giving a verbal command to the elephant, which would lower its trunk for the Mahout to climb aboard, from where it would raise him to a position where he could climb onto his seat. We experienced some exciting sightings and confrontations, mostly in the form of Short-horned Rhinos. When flushed, they would often make short, mock charges at the elephants, before crashing off through the tall grass.

I was dead keen to see a tiger close up, as were all the party members. Suddenly I heard this sort of growling noise, but couldn't make out from which direction it came. A few minutes later, I heard it again, so I tapped our Mahout on the shoulder. Fortunately, he could speak English, and I told him about the noise I had heard. He gave a bit of a chuckle, then he said, "What you heard were the stomach rumblings of the elephant." After that, I just sat back and tried to keep a low profile.

17.

I Will Not Complain

While I was living on Kangaroo Island, in the 1980s, I had a visit from a bloke by the name of Anthony Willoughby. He was an Englishman who had been brought up in various parts of Africa, and who now resides in Tokyo, Japan. Prior to arriving he had phoned me, saying that he wanted to discuss a special charter trip for some Japanese people. He spent a couple of days with me, during which time we laid out plans for an eleven-day trip, in August that year.

Basically, my brief was to pack as much action and adventure into eleven days, but with no danger to the clients. That last bit had me a bit concerned, as I had some fairly radical ideas in mind. They were paying a lot of money for this charter, and I wanted to make sure that they got their money's worth. In the end, I rang Anthony's business partner, Guy Cihi, who was putting up most of the money, to put a few ideas to him. He said "Go for it man," which was all that I needed.

Anthony ran a business called "I Will Not Complain, International." In Tokyo, they had a club called the "I Will Not Complain" Club and it was from the membership that their clients were selected. These were mainly Japanese business executives, from all walks of life, and the proviso was that, under no circumstances whatsoever, could anyone complain about anything that happened to them on any trip, worldwide. Well! That suited me just fine.

I put together an interesting, albeit unusual itinerary, and in due course, the party arrived at Adelaide Airport. A pea soup fog shrouded the airport, unusual for South Australia at that time of year. My mate Stoney, who was working the trip with me, and I, met a group of eight very jaded Japanese, a female American interpreter, Anthony Willoughby and Guy Cihi. We loaded them all into my International ex-Army Blitz truck, and headed northeast for the Murray River between Waikerie and Morgan. The Japanese had no inkling of the itinerary at this stage.

I had previously organised another mate, Ralph Ohlmeyer from Waikerie, to build a large raft, and to float it down to Markaranka Station. The fog was just lifting, and the party's first sight of anything in Australia, was this platform tied to the riverbank. It had a framework of two inch galvanised pipe, timber bearers, and a floor made from old packing cases. For flotation, it used 18 forty-four gallon drums. The floor covered an area of twenty-one feet by sixteen feet.

We loaded people and gear on board, and attached an Avon inflatable dinghy to the raft. This was to be a "living off the land" segment of the trip, and my stores reflected this as they contained only a bag of spuds and a pack of steaks. Stoney and I had a couple of shotguns and a 303 rifle; this was a very Spartan affair. We gave each of the Japanese a plastic paddle, and organised them into port and starboard parties. They couldn't speak much English, so most of the talking was through the interpreter.

We had a Mallee pole attached to the centre of the raft as a flagpole, and attached to this pole was an Australian flag. I have to admit that Stoney and I were still somewhat biased against the Japanese, remembering the old adage that says "you ignore history at your peril." One of the Japanese passengers asked if he could fly a couple of Japanese Club flags on the pole, so I said, "yes, as long as they are below the Australian flag." Not a good attitude you might think, but that was about to change.

We set off, drifting down the river on a fair current. We instructed the Japanese that when I yelled "port!" the port side party would paddle like buggery and the same for the starboard side. After a bit of observation, Stoney and I drew some interesting comparisons between the Japanese and Australian cultures. When organised with a leader, the Japanese were formidable on the paddles, but when the leader was absent or inoperative, they weren't much chop, seeming unable to organise themselves, or to appoint another leader. Australians on the other hand, particularly the country-bred variety, are just the opposite. They will tolerate a leader, especially if he or she is a good "bloke", but if the leader disappears, someone steps up to fill the gap, and the show goes on. When organised, the Japanese were very efficient paddlers, but this cannot always be. I think it gives a clue as to why the Australians were victorious in the Islands during the war.

We rounded a bend and drifted past an ex-serviceman blockie, with his family, cooking a barbecue on the river's edge. He called out; "Where have your mob come from?" I called back "Saigon." The family seemed duly impressed and stuck for words.

That evening we camped on a large sand spit near the edge of the river, and set about preparing a feed of large steaks and potatoes, a rare and expensive delicacy for the Japanese. Whilst this was happening, it was decided to find nicknames for each of the Japanese, as we were having much difficulty in remembering their real names. We chose to name them after birds, eg Heron, Ibis, Barn Owl, Sparrowhawk, Wood duck, Pelican, Egret and Magpie. After some time, we observed the one that we had dubbed Sparrowhawk, was moping about, and was obviously very upset. I asked the interpreter to explain Sparrowhawk's problem, and she explained that it was my fault. Apparently, the word Sparrow is very demeaning in Japanese culture. I called him over, and producing a bird book, showed him a picture of a Sparrowhawk, explaining through the interpreter that this was a bold and courageous hunter. The change that came over Sparrowhawk was amazing. He stuck out his chest, and strutted away a new man. I'm sure that many of this world's problems are due to misunderstandings.

It became dark and the steaks were ready for serving, but no diners were present. They were out on the river flat, staring up at the brilliant night sky, because this was a perfect Riverland evening, clear and dry. I explained to the interpreter that their steaks would be ruined if they didn't soon come, but she replied that they had never before seen stars. Stoney and I were amazed at this fact, and were duly humbled. I think that it was from this moment that our attitudes towards these people began to change.

There were still two more days on the raft, and by and large, our stores now consisted of a bag of spuds and not very much else. So our main focus now was on food gathering. Earlier that morning, we had scrounged a couple of dozen oranges from under some trees as we floated past a fruit block. About mid morning, with a more substantial feast in mind, we pulled into shore and split into two parties, each searching for bush tucker. We were mostly after witchetty grubs (the Red Gum variety that could be extracted with a length of wire), mushrooms and reed shoots. After an hour or so, we ended up with several hat-fulls of mushrooms and some reed shoots (the white bottoms), but we had no luck with the grubs.

Later that afternoon we made another stop, this time adjacent to a large Lignum swamp, our intention being to bag a feed of ducks for the evening meal. Stoney and I took off in different directions with our shotguns at the ready. We must have made a comical sight as each of us had a "tail" of Japanese, following along behind, Nikons poised and ready to shoot.

My foray was relatively straightforward, and I managed to bag a couple of Wood Ducks. Stoney, however, had a bit more drama. He shot a few more ducks, but on his way back to the raft, managed to walk into a wet "crab hole", and disappeared to his waist in sticky black muck, much to the delight of his camera-clicking tail. The crew seemed to get great pleasure from plucking and dressing the ducks, and they all ate well that night.

The final day on the raft saw us pass the Cadell Ferry crossing, so I called "Gooday!" to the Ferry Operator. His only retort was "Bloody Hell! I thought you were a load of shit with a big mob of rats on it." I thought this bloke's perception was a bit extreme, but it takes all types. I hope we made his day. By this time, we were becoming a very happy little group, despite the language problem, with both English and Japanese conversations taking place simultaneously.

As we approached Morgan, we came upon a wide reach of dead water, with very little flow. This presented us with a problem, but as if by magic, a large motor cruiser appeared. We hailed it and asked the occupants for a tow, an operation that was very nearly our undoing, as the retired gentleman/skipper executed a power take-off that submerged the front of the raft. All on board the raft acted like rats, and moved hurriedly to the rear, thus stabilising our vessel. The only casualty from this experience was a wet half bag of spuds.

A couple of kilometres out of Morgan, we unhitched from our rescuers, and drifted into the town. I had been considering the problem of finding somewhere to dispose of our giant craft, and had not yet come up with a solution. You can't just leave something like that around a river port, especially if you want it back some time. Then I had an idea. We pulled up against the grassed area between the historic old wharf and the ferry landing, and proceeded to tie up. While Stoney took the party up to one of the Morgan pubs for a beer, I walked down to a houseboat operator that I knew, from whom I had once hired a houseboat.

His name was Barry, and he was a bloke that liked to do a deal, so when he saw me and said, "Where did you spring from?" I told him that I had brought a party of 13 down the river on a large vessel. I told him that, if he was prepared to berth this vessel for up to two years, he could hire it out and keep all of the proceeds. Barry tried, unsuccessfully, to keep the disbelief out of his eyes. It wasn't every day that such good fortune floated into his patch. I made sure that the deal was locked in, and we took off in his ute to inspect the said craft. Upon catching sight of it, Barry couldn't contain himself, and I braced myself for his reaction. We arrived at the grassed area and looked out across the river. "Well! Where is it?" he asked, to which I replied "Right in front of you." On the other side of the river was a small motor cruiser tied up. "You mean that one over there?" he asked. "No" I replied, "I mean this one here," pointing at the half of the raft that was visible, sticking out in front of us.

It is not desirable that I record here, verbatim, his reaction, but let me just say that he was less than impressed, and he used some very colourful language to impress on me the extent of his disgust. I thought I was on a lost cause, but you can never tell just which way some people will jump. "Come on" he said, "I'll have to go and tow it home." I held my breath as he dropped me off at the pub and said a curt goodbye. Ten minutes later, as I watched through the bar window, he roared up in his speedboat, and with a cable attached to the raft, he dragged it down to his complex, like an angry ant hauling a huge crumb to its hole. True to his word, he looked after it for nearly two years. I don't think he hired it out at all in this time.

My Blitz had been delivered to Morgan by Alf Porter, the manager of Markaranka, so we loaded up and took off out across the Mount Mary Plains, heading for Burra. I intended to introduce our party to that Australian phenomenon, the counter tea, so we pulled up at a hotel in the centre of town. Burra, with its rich copper mining history, is a town built of stone, like most of the old South Australian country towns, and the pub was no exception. The locals in the bar made the Japanese very welcome, and very soon afterwards, a good mate of mine, Matt Riley arrived, and further improved the ambience of the occasion. I had a bit of trouble extracting the crew from there, and perhaps you couldn't blame them for wanting to stay. A counter tea in Burra might have been perceived as being a bit more substantial than living off the land on a Murray raft.

We drove off into the night, not a murmur of complaint coming from our party. Mind you, I wouldn't have heard one anyway, isolated from the rear section as I was, in the front cab. Up through Peterborough and Oodlawirra to Yunta, on the Broken Hill road, before turning north onto a dirt, station road. At about midnight I pulled up, told the party to go horizontal, and did the same myself. The last thing that I heard was Stoney yawning, and remarking that it had been a fair day at the office.

We were up before breakfast, boiled the billy, had a Spartan breakfast, and headed north into the dawning day. This was a morning that, I think would forever, remain etched into the minds of our Japanese companions. The season was good, and the countryside was wall-to-wall wildflowers. As the sun came up over the horizon, the Japanese were treated to a truly unique Australian spectacle, a spectacle that ranks as one of the world's greatest wildlife shows. There were literally thousands of red kangaroos, for as far as the eye could see, as thick as I had seen them for many years; so thick that the whole countryside appeared to be on the move. There were also scores of Emus, and plenty of varied birdlife, with the magnificent background of yellow billy buttons, white daisies, yellow-top, wild hops, and whole flats covered with the incredibly beautiful sturt desert pea, the floral emblem of South Australia.

Looking back at their faces, I noticed that they appeared to be in a sort of suspended animation or trance. Nothing could have prepared them for such a sight, a fact that Stoney and I felt very pleased about. Lunch on this day was prepared and eaten amongst a massive flat of Desert Peas, and a memorable lunch it was too.

We were heading for Angepena station, in the Flinders Ranges, to camp in the vicinity of an old goldmine. Here the party would have the opportunity to try their hands at a bit of prospecting. Friends of mine, Sid and Faye Nicholls owned this station, and I had made some interesting arrangements with their son, David, for that evening, and for the next morning. That evening, as part of our arrangement, David was to take his swag and his high-powered rifle, to camp on top of a very large hill overlooking our camp. May sound a bit ominous, but this was that sort of trip.

Following the longest water course in the Flinders Ranges, Frome Creek, I ended up camping a couple of kilometres short of the gold mine, intending to try a bit of panning for gold in the creek, which was still running in this good year. After the camp had been set up, Stoney took his 303 rifle, and followed by his entourage, headed off for a bit of goat shooting.

I thought I was alone in the camp, and after hanging up an old shearer's kettle in a native Pine tree, I began to peel some onions. Suddenly Yamaguchi appeared, carrying a small case. He was the oldest member of the party, and he could speak a little English. Giving me a little bow, he said, "Mr Rex, ah, do you mind, ah, if I practice trumpet?" Now my youngest daughter, Kate, was currently learning to play the clarinet, and her practice sessions were events that I usually tried to remove myself from. However, I said to him, "Sure Yamaguchi, (he didn't have a bird alias), but maybe you should go up the creek a little way." With a smile all over his face, he thanked me and headed off up the creek. In the meantime, I got back to the serious business of peeling onions.

Several minutes later, I heard a delightful trumpet sound floating down through the Pines and the River Gums. I recognised the theme from Exodus and Joey's Song, so I yelled out for him to come back to the campsite, apologising for my having banished him to the bush. The notes must have reached the heights because Stoney, himself a keen musician and dancing man, arrived back at the camp without any goats. For the remainder of the trip, Yamaguchi had a jazz slot before each evening meal. What a musician he turned out to be, playing almost any request by ear; a truly wonderful gift.

Next morning, we had to time our departure to the very second, and I hoped that my man on the mountain hadn't slept in. I'd spoken to the interpreter, and had asked her to instil into the minds of the Japanese, that we were on a bit of a sticky wicket, camped where we were. I told her to tell them that there was a half-mad old prospector in the area, who didn't take too kindly to anyone else in his patch, but I said that it was unlikely that we would bump into him. Very skilfully, she sowed that little seed, such that it was deep in the back of their minds. So it was that at exactly a quarter to eight we were ready to go, and I had started to load the people. There was already a couple inside with the rest on the steps, and queued up behind; they love queues.

I then took off my hat and scratched my head, the prearranged signal for David, up on the mountain. Suddenly there was pandemonium, as all hell broke loose. Kerbang – clang and the old kettle flew out of the Pine tree with a hole in it. More shots, then a spectacle that I will not forget in a hurry. You know what it's like when you almost tread on a snake's tail, when the rest of it's out of sight? It suddenly whips away and disappears in an instant? Well! That's just how the Japanese crew performed. One moment they were there, and the next they were nowhere to be seen, totally out of sight in the truck.

More shots, with pieces of Pine tree flying into the air. Stoney and I jumped into the truck, and I hit the starter. Stoney grabbed his 303, hung out of the window and let a couple of shots go up the mountain, and as I swung the Blitz around in a tight circle, I fired half a dozen shots from my revolver. (Author's note: *Before the reader starts to condemn the writer for irresponsible behaviour, this scene was carefully planned and discussed with David beforehand. He was quite safe, having concealed himself behind some very large boulders*). It must have looked pretty convincing from the back, although the cobs probably couldn't see us from under their seats.

It took five minutes to sort out our composure, before I was game to stop the truck. I jumped out and went around to the back, where I hopped up to have a look in the back. Most of the Japanese were still on the floor, but were gradually trying to resume their seats.

A Disorganised Retreat

The funniest thing was that their faces were almost completely devoid of any expression. One definite change in their appearance was very noticeable; they were all as white as Corellas. I made some reassuring noises, assisted by the interpreter, and they all seemed very pleased to be leaving the area. Later that afternoon in camp, I asked the interpreter how they had stacked up with that little drama. She told me that a couple of them had twigged, but had decided to enjoy the joke themselves, and not let on to the others. The rest more or less accepted that this sort of thing could happen in the Land of Oz, and put it down to experience.

This trip had already attracted some media attention, and I wasn't sure what sort of repercussions might be in store for us, if one of the journalists asked one of the party, "What was your most exciting experience on the trip?" Perhaps it could get a bit tricky.

We had driven to a location south of Blinman, to where one of my Cameleers was waiting with seven camels. The next couple of days were very pleasant, with an uneventful camel trek, through some of the best scenery that the Flinders Ranges has to offer. Like most people, the Japanese had a great fascination for the camels, sometimes just walking up and placing their hands on the animals' shoulders. After we said goodbye to the camels, we drove south and around the bottom end of Lake Torrens, the world's longest salt lake. Earlier that year I'd got a party together, and had made a south to north crossing of this lake by boat, full for the first time in history. The Flinders Ranges had received their highest rainfall ever, resulting in this unique situation. Now there was still plenty of water in the southern, deeper end of the lake, and I had a couple of boats on top of the Blitz, for just this occasion.

We made our camp on an attractive little Native Pine peninsula, and prepared the boats for a half-day trip along the southern shore. About an hour into the trip, the wind increased in strength, forcing us into the shore. We got out and had a walk around, and later when the wind had lessened, we headed back to camp in the boats. The most interesting facet of this part of the trip was the attractive scenery of this area; sand dunes with Native Pine, Mulga and other vegetation, with a large bluff as a backdrop. Looking across the blue water of the lake, the Ranges stood out in stark relief, a truly beautiful slice of Outback South Australia. Throughout the day I let it be known, a couple of times, that we were out of tucker, and just let that bit of information sink in. Arriving back at camp, we loaded the boats and then, instead of getting stuck into the meal preparation, Stoney and I sat around and had a beer. We knew that the Japanese were curious about the situation but their expressions did not reflect this.

Then, at about an hour before sundown, we heard the sound of an approaching aircraft. Suddenly a chopper swung around the bluff, did a quick circuit of the camp, and put down near the Blitz. Out hopped a man in white, wearing a chef's hat, who helped the pilot to carry polystyrene boxes of gear over to our table. Inside ten minutes, we had laid out before us, a gourmet meal of crayfish, prawns, poultry etc, along with a range of sweets that included pavlova and chocolate mousse. To cap it all off, a dozen bottles of chilled champagne were also unloaded and placed on the table. Once again, the expressions didn't reveal the true impact of this vision, but the interpreter recognised that they were "blown away" by it all. It also made a very pleasant change for Stoney and me.

Next morning there were chopper rides around the lake, before we loaded up the Blitz for the trip back to Adelaide. We didn't hear one word of complaint come from the back of the truck, all the way back to the city.

18.

Raining Red Rain

For many years I had a regular safari, with a group comprised mostly of members of the Melbourne bar, judges, barristers, solicitors etc, accompanied by their wives, some of whom were lawyers.

I used to look forward to these trips for a number of reasons. In consultation with the party, we would always select exciting locations. Even though these were 4WD vehicles and not camel trips, we experienced a lot of country that few other Australians ever see. They were always very lively trips, full of humour and repartee. On this occasion, a tract of country some six hundred kilometres west of Port Hedland, in the Great Sandy Desert, was about to be gazetted as a National Park, and was to be called the Rudall River National Park, one of the remotest in Australia. Because the party only ever had 14-15 days available, (the July legal recess) we would usually drive to the location nearest to our area of operation, and they would fly in from Melbourne, in this case to Port Hedland.

Prior to the commencement of these trips, one of the barristers would phone me to discuss the supply of alcoholic beverages. Although, I always supply a certain amount, the party always puts in a very substantial private order of beer, wines, port and muscat. On previous occasions, they had always taken McLaren Vale Wines, from where I was born and bred, as I was pretty parochial regarding the area, and had good arrangements with local wine makers. I was therefore somewhat taken aback, when the Barrister in question informed me that the party had decided to order from a very well known and respected Victorian winery. I let him know that I wasn't happy, but they were paying for it, and had set their minds on it. The liquor was to be sent over to Adelaide, and then out to my depot at McLaren Flat.

My party had to leave around a week before the safari departed from Port Hedland, and there were to be four vehicles. Three of these were from South Australia, and the other was a hired Toyota 4WD, Hi-Lux ute from Carnarvon, with Tom Kitchen driving. Bill Oliver was driving his Toyota station wagon, and I had my old Troop Carrier, with its specially designed roll up canvas sides. Stoney, from Darke Peake, was to meet us at Port Augusta in his Land Rover wagon. Patti and my girls, Georgi and Kate, who were thirteen and eleven respectively, were coming as far as Port Hedland, then returning home by air and coach.

We duly loaded our vehicles onto flat tops at Pt. Augusta, on the Indian Pacific express, and then settled down to a relaxed couple of days across the Nullarbor Plain to Perth. Bill had the majority of the Victorian wine casks, under a tarpaulin on his roof rack.

Our journey west was very enjoyable, as the Indian Pacific is one of the world's great trains. After we unloaded, we set off on our route which headed North. That morning I pulled up, about seventy kilometres out, next to some dead bush timber. As Bill and Stoney will testify, I've got a bit of a thing about wood. I never like to be caught without it, particularly with a party on board. Stoney ended up with what appeared like an abandoned eagles nest on his roof rack, and so we continued on.

The reason I had given us a week to get to Port Hedland, was to include a reconnaissance into Steep Point in Shark Bay. The following year (1988) I had a West - East camel crossing of the Continent planned, from the most westerly point, Steep Point, to the most easterly, Cape Byron in N.S.W. I needed to see what the terrain was like, plus some other factors, so it was late that afternoon when we were at Carrarang Station, talking to Mervyn Cliff. Big black clouds were rolling in across Shark Bay, and we set off for Steep Point as rain began to fall. The trip into the Point is mainly over very large white coastal sand dunes, through thick coastal bush and heath.

Soon it was raining in bucket loads, almost torrential. Because the track was sandy, we were not stopped although, at one stage, Bill's Toyota fell into a hole, and we had to winch him out, the three of us getting totally drenched in the process. After some three hours, we finally reached Steep Point, or we presumed so anyway. It was around midnight, as the track suddenly stopped near a cairn of stones, by a sheer cliff, and the rain kept on tumbling down. The Ellis family somehow rolled swags out on top of boxes of stores in the back of the Troopie, and had a fair sleep. None of us got out of the vehicles that night; correction - someone must have, as there was a very large foreign object next to one of my wheels, which seemed to lack an owner. I was sure none of us had ventured out and Bill and Stoney said the same. The supernatural is never far away. Next morning the rain had stopped, and a dramatic spectacle confronted us. Steep point juts out into the sea, with the historic Dirk Hartog Island guarding the waters of Shark Bay, its southerly tip only a couple of kilometres from Steep Point.

We had a surprisingly uneventful trip back to the bitumen, later learning that the area had received four inches of rain that night. We called at Hamlyn Poole Station where we met Brian and Mary Wake. This was to be the start of a long friendship, over a number of both camel and vehicle trips. About mid morning, we were on the Great Northern Highway again, heading for Carnarvon. I was up the front, Bill a kilometre back, and Stoney bringing up the rear in his usual spot. We had the C.B. radios on, and after a silence of ten minutes or so, Bill suddenly said "Rex, are you getting any rain up there?" I thought it was a funny question, because there wasn't a cloud in the sky. "No" I replied. "Well, its raining red rain back here, and my wipers can't keep up with it!' I pulled over, and Bill pulled up alongside, his window wipers going full bore, and his windows awash with red fluid. 'Don't tell me' I thought, as I hopped out of my vehicle, Stoney pulling up behind me. Sure enough, my worst fears were confirmed; the Victorian casks were weeping. In the short term, it was pretty funny, but I was more concerned about the long term.

The Seeping Casks

After a hasty conference, we decided on a desperate plan, and drove briskly to Carnarvon. It was a Sunday but nevertheless, drove around to the huge supermarket where, with a bit of luck, we managed to strike the boss, who was working back. I asked him if he had any one-gallon polythene water containers, and he thought he might have a couple. I said I needed at least twenty, and these were eventually in our possession. Then followed a frantic, re-containering of precious (and expensive) wines, ports and muscats. We were not so concerned about the port and muscat, but didn't care to dwell on the red and white wines situation. Despite the 'red rain,' we only seemed to have lost about three gallons altogether. We filled several 44 gallon rubbish drums up with grog-soaked cardboard, then we drove out, passing a 'wino' on foot, who was virtually speed walking toward the drums. He had been downwind, and was about to realize that all his birthdays had come at once. This was a Sunday that he probably would never forget.

We drove to the caravan park, after meeting Tom Kitchen in his Hi-Lux, and set up camp. We had a day and a half before the party flew in, a period that was fairly eventful, so we drove out of town about 6 kilometres, and dumped Stoney's load of wood at an isolated place on a bush track. This was for the first night's camp, soon after we picked up the party, and I knew we would be camping where there was little firewood. We then returned and proceeded to clean out the vehicles. We stacked all the grog alongside the vehicles, (approx thirty casks/poly containers, and fifteen cartons of canned beer); it looked pretty impressive. Just then, a retired couple walked past, and the old bloke stopped, looked at the beer, then at us and said, "You boys like a drink, do you?" We didn't think it was worth attempting an explanation. That load of casks had not only endured a jolting trip across Australia, on what is known to be a rough railway line, but it was only the curtain raiser, compared to the mad scramble over the sand dunes to Steep Point. Our party knew about the rail trip, but not of the Steep Point diversion.

Next morning we decided to just check on our wood supply, and just as well we did, for unbeknown to us, the track where we dumped it happened to lead to an Aboriginal settlement. It had all gone! Some Aborigines must be still thanking their lucky stars, although they seem to take both good fortune and misfortune in their stride, not like us buggers. Stoney couldn't believe it, he had carried that load for about two thousand kilometres for nothing. We still had three hours before the plane came in, and after yet another desperate conference; we sped into Hedland and commenced driving around until we found a building site. We then gathered off-cuts of sawn timber, and soon had a good load on Stoney's roof again.

I then put Patti and the kids on a plane to Perth, and soon after that, our party landed. After the usual greetings, we loaded up and drove out to a camp spot that I had selected. I then had to explain why most of the wine was contained in such an unorthodox fashion, and what my ten minute explanation really boiled down to, was a sort of 'I told you so!' I said that McLaren Vale casks are well known for their strength, but that it was obvious that the Victorian product wasn't as well encased. Bill and Stoney looked earnestly on, as there seemed to be a sort of a rage building in the group, but as far I could tell, it wasn't directed at us, it was aimed at the Victorian Wine Company. I felt a bit guilty, but got around that thinking that the said winery was a lot bigger than me, and would hopefully weather the terrible storm that would soon be unleashed.

We had a very good trip, and surprisingly, the red and white didn't seem any the worse for wear, even at the end of the trip. But imagine this. When our friends returned to Melbourne, I happen to know that a most shocking tirade was rained down upon the said winery, with promises never to partake of their wares again. It could almost certainly be said that the winery has probably never ever had a complaint like this before.

*Author's note: Like state secrets, I feel that a reasonable amount of time has passed for this information to be released. It is hoped that the members of that little party can feel it in their hearts to forgive us blokes. Time heals most things (hopefully).

19.

Elle in Little Sahara

In the eighties, when I was living on Kangaroo Island, I had a phone call from a representative of the famous American magazine, *Sports Illustrated.* Apparently, each year, they feature a big article on swimsuits, and this year it was Australia's turn. I was asked to meet, with four camels, the photographic party and the models, at a location known as Little Sahara. This is an area of totally bare, white sand dunes, which extend inland for several kilometres on the southern coast of the island. When in amongst these dunes, one has the feeling of being in the middle of one of the world's major deserts, providing that the sounds of the sea and the crashing waves cannot be heard.

The models taking part in this photo shoot were Elle McPherson, just starting to make a name for herself, and Paulina, a famous Polish model. The man with the camera had just won the coveted Pulitzer Prize that year, for some of his photographic exploits. I thought then that this might be an interesting contract.

I selected four likely camels, including my big dark leader called Sam, a camel for all seasons. It took me two days to ride, leading the camel string, from the Ravine de Casoars, where I lived, on the northwest corner of K.I., to Little Sahara; this was to be a six-day contract. The ride was enjoyable, plodding along on empty roads and bush tracks, with my mind in neutral for a fair bit of the time. I wasn't carrying much baggage, just a swag and a couple of pack bags holding my tucker, so all the camels had riding saddles on their backs.

The first night I rode into a bush property called Montebello, owned by a friend of mine called Doug Seton. Doug had a caravan parked at the foot of a scrub-covered hill, and on the shore of a nice freshwater lake. He lived on the mainland, but spent a lot of time on the island, working as an apiarist. He was surprised to see me, and even more surprised when he learnt of my mission. I suspect that he was also more than a little envious.

After a pleasant evening's stay with Doug, I headed off next morning, arriving at Little Sahara at about four o'clock in the afternoon. Setting up camp, I unsaddled and hobbled the camels, letting them head off for a feed in the bush. I cooked myself something to eat, read by the fire for a while before rolling out the swag.

Next morning, at about nine o'clock, a mini bus arrived, loaded with about twenty people, mostly women concerned about the wardrobe department. There was also the very portly Pulitzer Prize winner, and of course, Elle and Paulina, two very friendly girls who showed a lot of interest in the camels. The sky, unfortunately, was overcast, and after a couple of false starts, the shoot was called off for the day, at about four o'clock in the afternoon. Nevertheless, I found it a very interesting day. One thing became very obvious to me, and that was the dislike, almost verging on fear, that the rest of the party felt for the photographer. Can't say that I liked him very much myself. He was ill tempered, sarcastic and bombastic, and according to one of the girls, not just because of the overcast weather.

Not Impressed

Next morning it was fairly cold for that time of year, but at least the sun was shining for some of the time. I was walking up to the location, leading the camels and talking to Elle and Paulina, who were both wearing bikinis. I suggested that they should ride the camels, to which they said that they would very much like to, but the Pulitzer man would fly into a rage if they were to do so. Elle said that he would accuse them of risking bruising, and spoiling the photographs, which she also said, was quite ridiculous. About four makeup ladies, who were on the job, could cover up any blemishes. I made a mental note that I should try to get him up onto Sam, who could chuck him off into the bush.

I think that Elle was earning only about one thousand dollars a day at this time, but I can see how models really earn their money. All day long, the models had to adopt various poses along Sam's bare back. They had countless changes of swimsuits, and more posing, with very little pause, apart from a short break in the morning, and about a half an hour for lunch. I had what some might call an interesting job, crouching in the sand on one side of Sam, armed with a supply of apples, so that I could encourage Sam to turn his head whenever he was required to. However, Sam is no fool, and he very often chose to disobey me. On these occasions, I would cop some mild abuse from the photographer, and on a couple of occasions, I felt like decking him, but I thought that might jeopardise my contract. I wasn't earning any one thousand dollars a day, but it still was a very good week's work.

I could see by their goose bumps (it was getting colder) that it wasn't all beer and skittles for Elle and Paulina, along with the continual haranguing from the man with the camera. Certainly wouldn't happen now; that bloke would find himself with a one-way ticket to nowhere, with a busted Nikon wrapped around his ears.

The shoot was finally completed, and the party soon packed up all their belongings and left. I was paid with a large wad of money, but on reflection, I probably would have done it for nothing, just for the experience. It actually put me off my Weetbix for weeks afterwards. I duly received a copy of the *Sports Illustrated* magazine, and although our man had apparently taken three thousand six hundred photographs, only two were used in the article. Makes me feel better when I waste a bit of film myself.

20.

The Red Flag

In the early sixties, when I had just finished my first jackerooing job on Lilydale station in the north east of South Australia, I had a short stint jackerooing on an upper southeast property, near the Coorong in South Australia. It was a six thousand acre property, running sheep and Angus cattle, managed by a bloke called John Wilkinson.

John and wife Jo, lived there with their two young children, Peter and Suzie (aged 5). On occasions, we would borrow a farm hand from a neighbouring property, called Peter Van Beusingham. John, an ex digger from New Guinea, ran the place with an army discipline, very efficient, and a stickler for detail. I had just come off a big northern sheep run, where we had a pretty laid back existence, so I had to reorganise my attitude somewhat.

The first day I was there, John was explaining his system to me, and one of the first things he enlightened me on was the flag system. At the back door of the house was a flagpole, but it didn't fly anything as frivolous as the Australian flag or the Union Jack; most of the time, a business like green flag could be seen fluttering at the top of the pole, a flag that meant that all was well. If a yellow flag was run up, it meant that I was required at the homestead, but to finish what I was doing, then come home. On the other hand, if the red flag was flying, I had to drop what I was doing, and go to the homestead as quick as I could. John fixed me with a steely stare and said, "The red flag will only be flown in the case of extreme emergency." I might add that the homestead was in a sort of hollow in the middle of the property, and the flagpole could be viewed through binoculars, from most parts of the place. I was instructed to check the flags regularly with my binoculars, which I had to carry at all times. That suited me OK, because I am a keen birdwatcher anyway.

Well the months went by in a fairly pleasant fashion, although I was missing the atmosphere of the north, and I felt I was going mouldy with the high rainfall of that year. I was also missing my mates a bit. John had given me an excellent miniature Kelpie that he bred, so I was enjoying the extra and varied sheep work to be had on an inside property. Every now and then, I would get a yellow flag, which tended to break the monotony of some jobs, but never a red one.

I did a lot of horse work down there, which meant that most days I would be riding. One overcast day I was doing some fencing, about three kilometres from the homestead, on the edge of the scrub. I sat down by a Yakka bush to have my smoko and picked up my binoculars and I was giving the country a wide sweep, looking for Raptors (birds of prey). When the homestead came into view, I had a second look, because something seemed different. Then it hit me like a sledgehammer between the eyes; the red flag was flying. I chucked a half-eaten peanut paste sandwich over my shoulder, jumped on my horse, and was off at the gallop with Tibun running behind, barking. John had a strict rule about galloping your horse unnecessarily, but no worries now. The horse knew it too, and was going like a cut cat. There was only one gate closed (a wire cocky gate) between the homestead and me, and I thought about it as I galloped along. This horse could jump a bit so I thought, 'Bugger it, we'll give it a go'. The gate appeared and I urged my horse on, not that she needed it, and over we went with a hoof clipping the top wire. We landed a bit rough, but we recovered and hammered on.

A lot of things were going through my mind at this time, wondering what the emergency was, but my speculations were cut short as the homestead appeared. The place looked like a morgue, with not even a chook in view. I pulled up with a flourish at the back of the house, prepared for any eventuality, and jumped off the horse. The back door opened and little Suzie came out with a beaming smile on her face. I soon found out that axe murderers were pretty thin on the ground, and that Suzie had decided to have a fiddle with the flags; she was home on her own for a short period. 'Interesting,' I thought, and just about then, John and Jo drove in, sporting very concerned expressions. John looked at my lathered horse, my buggered dog, the red flag and Suzie, and asked me what was the score. When he digested all that, he told me to hose my horse down, and disappeared inside with Suzie, where I believe a little corporal punishment may have been the order of the day. In any case, it was probably the most exciting day that I spent on that property.

Footnote: John retired some years ago, and every year he travels on at least one camel trek or expedition, where his valued services are much appreciated. We call him *The Old Cameleer*. He is just as disciplined as ever, and is in no need of a weekly thrashing.

21.

Douglas Scrub - A Wildlife Experiment

In the mid seventies, we purchased seventy-eight acres of land at McLaren Flat, which included about fifty acres of excellent bushland, mostly Pink Gums (*Eucalyptus Fasiculosa*), with a varied understorey. I had always had a keen interest in native fauna, and for a long time, had been aware that many of our small animals were either extinct, or on the verge of extinction. Apart from habitat destruction, the other reason for their demise was the toll taken by introduced feral animals, such as foxes, cats and rabbits. Governments had done nothing substantial in addressing this catastrophe, apart from setting aside areas like National Parks or Conservation Parks, whilst the chief problem of the feral predators and competitors remained. My idea was to totally feral-proof this area, get rid of all the feral animals, and to reintroduce, as near as possible, the original inhabitants.

The first job that I undertook on the property (I called it Douglas Scrub, after an old inhabitant) was to get a large trench excavated, forty metres long, by six metres wide, by three metres deep. After about six months, we had this trench almost completely filled with rubbish, including several old car bodies.

Apart from the scrub, the property comprised around twenty acres of old grapevines, growing on the rich flats along Douglas Gully Creek. There was also an old house where the original inhabitants, Dougie Ward, and his family, lived. Dougie was a well-known local character, who dearly loved a drop of port wine. This fact became evident, when we found a number of partly filled port bottles, sitting in natural "racks" in the century-old currant and shiraz vines. It was well known locally, that he used to walk the five miles into the McLaren Vale pub, reinforcing himself with tots of port, from caches that he had in the bush. After Dougie died, Alec Bell, a neighbour and keen naturalist, who knew of my interest in the property, told me that the property was to be auctioned. The sale was not widely publicised, and my father (the late Max Ellis) and I attended, and were successful in purchasing it. That was a very good day.

The original house was not 'do-uppable,' so we demolished it, and carted it off to the local dump. In the meantime, we had a temporary transportable building, set up in a clearing on the sandhill, with bush on three sides, and the Gum Creek at the bottom of the hill. A local builder, with me helping, shifted our large, fifty foot by thirty foot shed, from McLaren Vale, moving it in four sections, and reassembling it behind the house; no mean feat, but George Attrill was another sort of local legend.

While this was going on, I was putting my idea to the South Australian National Parks and Wildlife Service. I didn't have a lot of luck initially, but I kept chipping away, until finally I was put in touch with a bloke called Laurie Delroy. He could see merit in my idea, so things started to move after that. I was issued with a rare permit, which enabled me to trap certain species of native fauna, for reintroduction to Douglas Scrub. All this time, I was building the fence, sometimes on my own, and sometimes with local mates, while my good friend, Alec Bell, gave me lots of encouragement from next door, and eventually, Patti, Georgi and I moved into the little transportable. One day there was a knock on the door, and there stood the late Doug Collett, from Woodstock Winery, holding onto a huge yellow bucket, loaded with home-grown vegies, with a bottle of chilled champagne in the middle. You don't forget moments like those.

The posts for the fence I personally cut from Kuitpo Forest, as the Forester at the time was Alan Gray, a mate of mine, who let me loose in a block of regrowth Pine. The newly cut timber then had to be carted to Meadows, for treatment against termites. It was a great moment when the first strainer post went in. My fence design was simple but effective, having five feet of vertical wire netting, with three feet of netting, eighteen inches either side, on the ground and above the vertical netting, resembling the letter H on its side. The top stays to hold the wire, were similar to those used in vineyards.

Most of my wire netting was scrounged from old defunct Currant drying racks, and when I ran out of local un-rusted wire, Trevor Shiell, a mate of mine living in the South Australian Riverland, lined me up with more from his area. I did have to purchase many bundles of six-foot steel posts, plus a number of rolls of new netting, to put the finishing touches to the fence. I even had to install floodgates, with concrete aprons, in three places where creeks passed through the enclosure, but finally it was completed. I'm not sure how much this fence cost me, as I didn't take account of my labour, but somehow it just didn't seem to matter, completion was so very satisfying.

During these first eighteen months, I had a local contractor, by the name of Murray Oates, come in to clear and burn all the grapevines. I then planted about eight acres of pine trees (*Pinus Radiata*) on the Southern flats, with a double row of Tasmanian Blue Gums along the road hopefully to protect the pines. I'm no lover of Radiata pines, but my intention was to harvest them in ten years or so, as a cash crop, and to then plant local native flora. I also planted several thousand endemic native trees, shrubs and ground cover, throughout all the other open ground.

We constructed a large dam, where Douglas Gully and Blewett Springs Creeks adjoined, complete with a small island. Nearby I constructed viewing platforms, connected with a boardwalk, over a small wetland, overlooking the dam. George Attrill and I also commenced to build a local stone and pine, log house, in front of the transportable. It had a courtyard in the middle, with Mintaro slate throughout, including the verandahs (I carted that slate from Mintaro in the Camel truck), and a cellar was dug under one of the verandahs, a feat that was not without drama.

The house was almost complete, except for this cellar. The excavation, under a side verandah, was covered over with large sheets of flooring material, with a tarpaulin over the top, and was laid out with other materials around, so it did not look too conspicuous. Well! We were working there one, morning when George let fly with some robust comments that I won't try to reproduce here. What he was trying to convey to me, was the fact that the building inspector was driving over the newly constructed Blue Gum bridge, and was heading our way. We had nothing to hide but the cellar, which was a late idea; well after the building plan was submitted and approved.

I knew that to submit a revised plan that included the cellar, would delay the building project by months. At that time, building inspectors were as rare as Pink Robins, and this "rare bird" was only seconds away, catching us completely flat footed. Our outward appearance was, hopefully, one of casual nonchalance, but underneath the surface, my nerves were like the strings of a Spanish guitar. I wasn't sure about George, but guessed that he was thinking that the cellar might have an early occupant if it was discovered.

We exchanged the false pleasantries under these circumstances, and watched as the inspector moved through the house. He was moving toward the covered cellar, and finally ended up standing on top of the bloody thing. Like a nail drawn to a magnet, he seemed to settle there as though he was comfortable. To no avail, George and I tried walking off, talking as we went, trying to get him to follow. I eventually moved him, by asking him about some non-existent problem, at the other end of the building. When he finally drove off, we sat down and had a cuppa, a most enjoyable smoko. When we'd finished the cellar, we sold the transportable.

I had been systematically shooting and trapping foxes, but knew that there were many still left in the scrub. One weekend, I assembled around twenty blokes, armed with shotguns, to hopefully, walk through in sight of each other, to complete the fox eradication. Bruce Rayner, an ex Vietnam veteran and expert marksman, took up position on the roof of an old currant drying shed, out in the open. I had a small army, mainly kids, carrying sticks and buckets, acting as beaters, and walking behind the shooters. It was quite a performance when we started, and most of the resident wildlife probably suffered nervous tension for the next week. A few Western Grey Kangaroos were put up, but no foxes. Just before the long line of shooters emerged from the bush, we heard a shotgun blast, above the din of the beaters. A fox had broken cover in front of us, heading straight for Bruce, on top of the shed. This was quickly despatched, making it one fox, the sum total. The day finished with a keg and a barbecue, up by the house.

I was not certain that no foxes or cats remained within the enclosure, but my worst fears were realised when, a fortnight later, I saw the tracks of two foxes. I worked out a plan to dispose of these creatures, though without much confidence, as I know just how incredibly smart foxes can be. I got hold of some half-rotten meat, and took it down near Alec's gate, to where I'd seen the tracks. After dark I scattered it around there, and then set five rabbit traps within a five-foot radius circle. That night I went to bed, not expecting too much of a result just yet.

I was awakened from my slumber at about one o'clock in the morning, by the sound of the frenzied barking of my Blue Heeler. I climbed wearily out of bed, picked up a torch, and hastened down to where I'd set the traps. I couldn't believe my luck. Before me I saw not one, but two large foxes in the traps. Not without a little sympathy, I despatched the foxes, which proved to be a dog and a vixen. It appeared that the dog had been caught first, and the vixen had come to investigate, becoming trapped as she did, but only by one foot. If I hadn't arrived straight away, she would have bitten off that foot and escaped. It gives me no joy, killing living animals, but I had a very real sense of satisfaction that night.

Careful, regular checking over the next month didn't reveal the presence of any more feral animal tracks. Every two days I would walk the perimeter, checking the fence, and on occasion, filling in places where foxes were attempting to gain entry, by digging under the wire. At last, we were ready to commence the introduction of some native animals.

Some of the first residents were Tammar Wallabies from Kangaroo Island, along with four Cape Barren Geese with clipped wings. In a small enclosure, I had several pairs of Banded Land-rails, a bird that I hoped would recolonise the reed bed areas along the creeks.

I contacted an old school mate of mine, David Wotton, long before he became a prominent State Politician. David had a large tract of thick bushland, up at Forest range, where there was one of the few known colonies that remained in the hills, of Short-nosed Bandicoots. We set our Elliott traps on his property, over several weeks, and caught, as well as several pairs of bandicoots, bush-rats and the small, local, Yellow-footed Antechinus. These were all released into the enclosure, with quite a lot of publicity from the *Advertiser*. As far as I knew, this was the only such experiment operating in Australia at that time. At about the same time, John Wamsley was preparing his degraded dairy farm at Longwood, in the Adelaide hills, for what was to become the world famous Warrawong Sanctuary.

When we were building the house, I asked George to construct a small vault, behind a loose stone in the wall of the courtyard. Into this vault I placed a few objects, including a bottle of red wine, a bottle of port, locks of the kids' hair, and a prediction of what the Ellis family would be doing in the year 2000. At the time of writing this, (March 1999) I am looking forward to opening that vault. An arrangement to make this possible was written into the document of sale, and agreed to by the purchaser when we sold the property.

In the summer, I kept my camels in the open area at the western end of the property, operating my day treks to the wineries, and to the Onkaparinga Gorge. I had been discussing with National Parks & Wildlife Service Officers, how to go about obtaining other animals that once frequented the region, particularly Numbats and Brush-tailed Bettongs, but for a variety of reasons, this was not going to happen for quite some time. We had spent almost five years at Douglas Scrub, and I suppose that I was becoming impatient with the fact that I could not increase my number of species.

After a short holiday on Kangaroo Island, we decided that we should move over there to live, which would mean that we would have to sell Douglas Scrub, but I decided to keep the 12 acres of cleared area for my summer camel depot. I was determined to sell to a sympathetic person or group, who would carry on the work that I had started. At one stage, the Government looked like purchasing it, but then decided against it. I knocked back another buyer who wanted to establish a golf course, and I eventually sold it to the Girl Guides Association for a lesser price.

Even though my fence was not electrified, it was nevertheless, very successful, if regularly monitored. This monitoring is absolutely crucial, as foxes will continually try to dig beneath the foot netting so, to be truly effective in the long term, electrifying the fence is the only answer. John Wamsley has established Warrawong Sanctuary, as a role model for his larger sanctuaries that are already operating. He has proven, without doubt, what is required to save our wildlife; Private enterprise has succeeded in doing what our State and Federal Governments should have done many years ago. Earth Sanctuaries continues to grow, and is now a publicly listed company, with feral-free sanctuaries operating, with others planned, at locations across the length and breadth of Australia.

A number of Earth Sanctuary properties have been purchased by the Australian Wildlife Conservancy, a private organisation based in Western Australia. They are carrying out this work, purchasing and feral-proofing properties of high conservation value throughout Australia.

Although our paths never crossed in those days, John Wamsley and I did share a few interesting parallels. At the same time as I was setting up Douglas Scrub, he was pursuing a sort of guerrilla warfare against feral pine trees. For years, they had been gradually infiltrating remnant bushland and roadsides, imposing a very un-Australian stamp upon the hills scenery. The Stirling Council had actually pursued an aggressive Europeanization, flora wise, of their arm of influence. John headed an enthusiastic, active group of people who called themselves GROPE, (Get Rid Of Pines) and much nocturnal activity saw the mysterious disappearance of many pine trees, cut off in their prime, so to speak. He became public enemy number one, as far as the Stirling

Another One in the Ground

Council was concerned. Many stories were being circulated, but they are not for me to tell.

At the same time, though, I had organised a group of like-minded mates, who became known as the midnight tree planters. In the course of our activities, a few pine trees 'disappeared' from the local landscape, so you could say that we were sort of unofficially affiliated with GROPE, but you would be battling to find any paper work. Our main objective was planting endemic natives along the roadsides, open spaces, and private properties, and we would often target properties that had over-cleared for the purpose of planting grapevines. Quickly learning by our mistakes, we would plant in close proximity to fence posts and other obstacles where the 'Grim Reaper' (the slasher) could not effect its deadly swathe. The evenings would generally start at a member's house, and over a couple of ports, we would plan the night's mission. On a number of occasions we would be forced to lie as flat as shadows, in order to avoid an embarrassing discovery. We felt as guilty as hell, like environmental vandals, instead of knights of the green gumleaf. Very satisfying activities though.

Sometimes we passed the hat around, for money to buy trees, but on a number of occasions, a local plant nurseryman called Brian Gould, would give us boxes of native tube stock. I've always been a tree planter and I still am. There's a lot of places in the McLaren Vale district where I can drive around, and appreciate some of our 'wild plantings'. I could instance the healthy-looking Spotted Gums on the lawn in front of the McLaren Vale Foodland, a 4am effort, undertaken by Bill Oliver and myself. Duffy Sigston was to assist us, but he arrived late, to find the trees in and us gone. The various owners of the Supermarket all presumed that someone else had planted them; this was our intention.

John Wamsley makes an art form out of opposing bureaucracy and Councils where stupidity prevails. I had a memorable skirmish where I suffered a physical defeat, but scored a moral victory, for what it's worth, when I owned Douglas Scrub. The fence alignment on Moritz Road simply followed the curve of the roadway, at the time still unsurveyed. The Local Council, based in suburbia, took exception to this, but I stuck to my guns and I appeared to have won the battle. Councils, however, have long memories it would seem. No sooner was the ink dry on the sale document, than the Council "pounced". They contacted the Girl Guides Association, and indicated that the eastern boundary fence was actually on Council property, and therefore would have to be moved. The Guides contacted my agent, complaining that there had been no encumbrances mentioned in the contract, so they felt that the liability was still mine. So it came back to me, and I was furious, but the bastards had me "snookered".

As a result, I took the story to the media, and they pounced upon it with relish. I had a field day with them, but I realised that I wasn't going to win this war. On one memorable day, I gathered together around thirty volunteers, and during the daylight hours, we dismantled about 250 metres of vermin proof fence, re-erecting it some few metres away from the original alignment. This caused traffic jams as onlookers crowded around. The best one-liner I heard all day was uttered by one of the neighbours, a retired airline pilot with his arm in a sling. A Channel 10 reporter asked him how he had broken his arm and he replied, "I was run over by a Council truck." Not true, but it certainly hit the spot.

The day after the new fence had been completed, I erected a huge hand-written sign, facing the roadway. The heading stated, "This is a Monument to Bureaucratic Mediocrity," and underneath was an outline of what had occurred. The local Strathalbyn newspaper gave it front-page coverage with the article and photographs. This must have incensed the Council, as a few days later, a mate of mine, who was in the bush near the fence, saw a Mini Minor van pull up. This van had Council signwriting on its side, and two Council employees jumped out. They literally tore the sign from the fence, and to my mate's amazement; they jumped up and down on the chipboard backing, breaking it into manageable pieces, and loaded it onto the roof of their van. They then roped it down and fled from the scene, as though with guilty consciences. So ended a pathetic saga, where bureaucracy won the day, but at a cost.

From my point of view, the Douglas Scrub enterprise did not end well. The Girl Guides Association went on to purchase the property, and seemed very keen to continue the concept. I stressed the absolute necessity of the regular checking of the fence, even offering the services of a mate, a dedicated fox hunter who would, for a nominal couple of dollars a week, guarantee the fence's security. This offer was declined, and sadly, within six months, foxes were back within the enclosure, and not far behind came the many noxious weeds that I had laboured hard and consistently to eradicate.

I know that there were many in the Association that deeply regretted the loss of this great opportunity (to inherit a feral-free property), but the body had other priorities. Money and many hours of voluntary labour have turned Douglas Scrub into a magnificent property, but to me, the most vital ingredient is missing. I am very proud however, of the fact that the Douglas Scrub project is officially on record, as being one of the earliest attempts to re-establish original native fauna. By excluding feral predators, this concept works, as is evidenced by the ongoing success of Earth Sanctuaries Pty. Ltd. In addition, even Government agencies are getting into the act.

22.

Big Night Out

One summer, in the 1980s, I decided to operate a Road Show; that is, a travelling film show to promote the business. It was to visit most South Australian regional areas, from the West Coast to the South East. I would operate some of it, with other of my casual safari leaders doing other regions. We travelled in the "Blitz", a specially designed safari vehicle, based on an ex Army International truck.

In this instance, there were three of us, and we had just completed two weeks of filming in various areas, including the York Peninsula.

Prior to the Road Show starting, I had made arrangements with various Lions Clubs in the relevant towns, to organise the venues and the local advertising for me. This meant that we were to just roll up at the town in question, usually in the mornings. We would meet our town 'agent', open up the hall, and set up the gear. The Blitz would be parked prominently in front of the hall, and the remainder of the daylight hours were free. This time was usually spent playing tennis, swimming, reading, or looking around the town. After the film night, we would camp in swags on the huge Blitz roof rack, usually at some nearby bush or beach location, on the way to our next town; not a bad life.

One Saturday morning, at the end of my particular stint, we saw an ad for a dinner dance at a York Peninsula Pub. We figured we were due for a night out, so we decided to attend, and in the early evening, we left the Blitz in front of the Pub with the canvas sides rolled up, and headed off to the dinner dance venue.

We secured a table and watched as the three-piece band set up. The day's temperature had been over the ton, and the beer was flowing freely. We had just ordered our first jug, when in walked my brother-in-law, Ken Smith. Ken's wife, his brother-in-law Roger, and his wife, accompanied him. Roger was a local farmer and Ken, also a farmer, was holidaying in a shack here.

Ken's group joined us, and we settled in for a long night. If the music is right then I'll dance all night, and tonight the music was good. The little combo played well, with the blokes only taking the odd break to revive themselves. Many jugs of "high octane" beer were consumed on this hot evening, as this was in the days before the arrival of light beer on the scene. I was dancing almost non-stop, and before we knew it, the time was two o'clock. The band then played their last medley as we downed our last beers.

I felt pretty lively at this time, but still quite in command of all my faculties. We were to drive a distance of around two kilometres to Ken's shack, where we would roll out our swags for the night. Just before leaving, I looked into the open back of the Blitz, and to my great annoyance, noticed that one of our swags had been "knocked off." The open truck was an open invitation to thieves, but I was really savage about it. It was decided that the girls should drive back to the shack in their car, while four of us, including Roger, who would show the way, squeezed into the cramped cabin of the Blitz

Now Roger is a good bloke, albeit a very correct one, especially in his Home Town. I make mention of this before we start, because if this was not the case, the following incident would not have occurred.

I hit the starter button and off we went. Perhaps it was because of the crowded cab (I like to think so) that, as I negotiated the sharp curve that immediately confronted me, a nearside, rear wheel jumped the kerb. This is what started Roger going. He said: "Hell! You don't want to do that." I thought to myself that this was a sort of unnecessary comment, but I held my tongue. "You want to be more careful," he said. Well! I've got to say, that did annoy me; on top of already being annoyed at the loss of the swag. I was driving alongside a large park with lawn and trees, and I said to him: "What do you think about this then?" As I spoke, I hooked the steering wheel left and mounted the kerb, rumbled across the park and headed for the other side. Roger was aghast. "You can't do that," he croaked. "I don't know," I said, "it seems pretty easy to me." The Blitz lumbered out the other side, over the footpath, and back onto the road.

Now I would have left it at that, if only Roger had swallowed his tongue, but no such luck. "You'll get us all hung" he yelled," you're mad as a cut snake." Well! By this time, I was beginning to enjoy Roger's outrage. I was approaching a series of railway crossings with stop signs, three of them in fact, two of which seemed to run into dead ends towards the wharves. The town appeared to be as dead as a morgue, so I proceeded to drive through the first stop sign. "Jeez, you're crazy," said Roger, as he tried to lower his profile, while the others were enjoying this little scenario. I drove through two more stop signs, and with Roger still protesting, approached a T-junction with a fairly steep bank, leading down to the railway line. I thought 'What the Hell' as I put the Blitz into four wheel drive, low range, and drove across the junction, and down the embankment. Anyone in the back with a cup of tea would have spilt it all at that moment. Roger was reduced to a series of squeaks, as the Blitz crept slowly down the bank towards the railway line. I then engaged reverse, and retraced my tracks up the bank towards the roadway. The old girl was getting a good workout tonight. Regaining the road, I decided to drive in a normal, sedate manner to our lodgings.

It was only then that I noticed, in my rear view mirror, the flashing blue light approaching. 'Oh! Hell' I thought. If I wasn't quite sober before, I reckon I was now. The police car came alongside, and a particularly predatory looking policewoman waved me over. Roger seemed to disappear under the rubber dust cover of the gear stick. Leaving the motor still running, I jumped down and walked around to the back of the truck, closely followed by the male and the female police officers. The lady looked formidable, but the bloke looked affable enough. Just then his hat fell off, which I thought was a bit unusual, so he picked it up and put it back on before addressing me. "Driver! Have you been drinking tonight?" he asked. I told him that I'd had a few, but that I'd danced a lot of miles as well. The lady cop just glared at me, like a Doberman ready for the kill. Then the male officer's hat fell off again, and that's when I thought I might have a fighting chance. As he picked it up again, I noticed the lady cop give him look of exasperation. "Driver!" he said "Up until we first saw you, we'd had a pretty quiet night. We were parked near the Pub when we saw you start up, and decided we should follow you when we saw you jump the kerb. Mind you, there's no law against jumping the kerb." He looked at me, for a few seconds, with an amused half smile on his face. (His partner was anything but amused). "Then I thought you must have dropped a tie rod." He chuckled, and his hat almost fell off again. "You left the road and disappeared into the park. I then proceeded around the park, like the vast majority of motorists do, just in time to see you reappear back on the road." He looked at me with interest. "Then you drove straight through three stop signs without stopping, and next thing," he said with a look of almost disbelief "you disappeared off the bloody radar screen."

The lady officer appeared furious, not enjoying this discourse at all. "I waited patiently," he said, straightening his hat "and my patience was rewarded, as you backed back onto the radar screen." I was finding his description pretty annoying, but inside I was slowly dying, as I anticipated two years in the safari business without a driver's licence.

Then the officer suddenly asked "What sort of a donk has she got?" I was taken aback momentarily, before telling him that it was a 354 Perkins.

"Lovely motor," he said, as I noticed the lady officer roll her eyes. Then he said, "Well! I think we'd better get you to blow into our bag," which the lady police officer snatched out of the patrol car, and thrust at me. I'd heard of these new devices, but I'd never been near one, so I wasn't too sure just where they wanted me to plug it in. "Blow in it," the lady hissed, and I did so. "Harder," she said, and I did. She took it from me, and peered at it, and then in annoyance she shook it, and looked at it again. "Must be faulty," she said, throwing it into the car. She scratched around in the back for a while, before reappearing with another one. I re-enacted the process, and as they both looked at it with disbelief, I thought the lady was going to burst a blood vessel. The male officer then said to me "Well Sunshine! You don't seem to be over the limit, however that doesn't mean that you're off the hook." He looked at the Blitz, then back at me, and finally he said "You'd be in a lot of trouble without a licence, wouldn't you?" I agreed very earnestly, assuring him that I most definitely would be. "Here's what I'll do. I'm going to book you for driving through a stop sign without stopping." His mate stared incredulously. "Now you get in that impressive old truck, drive very carefully to your place, and don't ever let me see you again." "Thank you officer," I mumbled, as I walked back and hopped up into the cab. Roger was, by this time, little more than a grease spot on the floor, and the others looked at me inquiringly. "Let's just say that I have more luck than I deserve," I said, as I drove, with great concentration, to Ken's shack.

Unwelcome Pursuit

23.

The Feast

In the mid 1990s, I was driving over to the Western Australian coast to start a 30-Day Transcontinental, a four-wheel drive safari that we sometimes do across Australia at its widest point. It stretches from Steep Point at Shark Bay in the west, to Byron Bay in New South Wales. On the way over, I was doing what we call a service run to the camel camp. The camel string had just completed a fourteen-day trek, with a party of birdwatchers; in the Pilbara region, and I had a party, in my 4WD OKA, that was about to join a forty-day expedition across the Gibson Desert. We were joined by a mate in Kalgoorlie, Ridge Warburton, and his four-wheel drive Land Rover, with extra people for the camel expedition, so we headed off, and duly reached the camel camp at a location on the edge of the Gibson Desert.

After a couple of confusing hours of transferring passengers and gear, we set off on a two-hour drive to Kumarina Roadhouse, on the highway between Newman and Meekatharra. The birding group, headed by Richard Jordan of Emu Tours, were old clients, who had chartered a number of our camel expeditions over the years. It was my intention to reward them with a special dinner that evening, at the roadhouse. Some weeks previously, I had contacted the manager, and explained that I required a meal, just a bit better than the average roadhouse meal, for which I was willing to pay $25 per head; there was to be a total of about eighteen people participating. The manager seemed very enthusiastic about the idea, and told me that it would serve as a dummy run, for a dinner that he was to prepare several weeks later, for a group of mining executives.

We duly arrived, and after the overworked showers stopped running, people headed for the dining room. A long table had been set up along one side of the roadhouse dining room, and it was very well presented. The only other occupants at the time, were two tough-looking truckies, wearing navy blue singlets. They were attacking, with single-minded concentration, two huge slabs of steak, so large that they hung over the edges of their plates. Our group seated themselves around the table, eagerly anticipating the meal. There were beers at every place plus numerous bottles of quality red and white wines that were lined up the length of the table.

The first course arrived, a liberal serving of oysters, upon which the party fell like crows at a road kill. The wine began to flow, and a cloud of conviviality pervaded the table. Ten minutes later, large bowls of fish soup were served, which also disappeared like a summer shower on a desert sand dune. This was quickly followed by a robust serving of seafood cocktail, accompanied by side plates of garlic bread. It began to dawn on me that we had well and truly exceeded our $25 per head's worth, and we had not even reached the main course yet. It was a nice feeling to know that this meal was pre paid, though I was getting curioser and curioser. Looking around the table, I noticed that the beneficiaries were slowing down considerably; a bit like a vehicle that was skimming along a bush track, suddenly striking heavy sand or mud. Definitely heavy going for some of them.

There was only a slightly longer wait, as the seafood cocktail bowls were cleared away. The main course was preceded by four of the staff arriving, each carrying three bottles of wine, that were ceremoniously uncorked, and lined up along the centre of the table. Looking again at a few expressions, I got the feeling that some of these people thought that they were on a gastronomic runaway vehicle, and wanted to jump off. The main course then arrived, and I noticed a couple of expressions that reflected unmistakeable horror; they were locked in, as it were. This was a special treat, and they couldn't run away from it, except for one bloke who was asleep, with a beaten look on his face. The rest of the crew bravely attacked (probably the wrong word) their plates.

For a little bloke, I'm not bad on the tooth, but I had been full, halfway through the seafood cocktail that was the size of some main courses. I do, however, have a very good stomach, and decided that, no matter what, I would see this thing through. The conversation at this stage, was no longer animated, in fact as the assembled made tentative inroads into the massive plates of mixed seafoods, (barramundi, calamari, prawns, moreton bay bugs etc. etc.) about the only sound was the taped background music. I noticed that, at one stage, "You load sixteen tons, and what do you get?" was coming through the loudspeakers. Various thoughts went through my mind, as I disposed of yet another seafood item, and I couldn't help thinking that maybe the mining executives' meal had been combined with ours. This thing just wasn't making any sense. I noticed that the truckies, sitting with their plates resembling salt lakes, were casting furtive, unbelieving glances in our direction.

Looking down the table, I noticed two other sleepers; one holding up his fork in mute protest, while others were looking definitely seedy. Moments later, a large lady pushed back her chair, hauled herself to her feet and staggered outside; she didn't reappear. By now, the truckies were steadfastly watching us, their television entertainment completely ignored.

When the remnants of the main course were cleared from the table, the occupants were not a pretty sight. Some had a look of disbelief on their faces, which turned to dismay, ten minutes later, as the sweets arrived at the table. These consisted of a combination of fruit salad and icecream, and pudding covered in caramel sauce. When the waitress asked the consumers for their choice, most seemed incapable of answering. About half a dozen of them were slumped in their chairs, making no attempt to start on their sweets, so I stood up, though with difficulty, and took six bowls of sweets over to the truckies, asking them if they were interested. The biggest one focussed his piggy little eyes on me, not sure if I was being a smart Alec or not. This was something totally outside his experience. He nodded his affirmative, so I surrounded him with fruit salad and caramel pudding. A slow, delighted smile began to crease the face of his mate, as he eagerly anticipated his windfall.

I then returned to the table of torment, and we commenced to make some sort of inroads into the dessert; a bit like a small corps of determined dung beetles, confronted by a massive mountain of manure. Only about half of the party were still going, and after the bowls were cleared away,

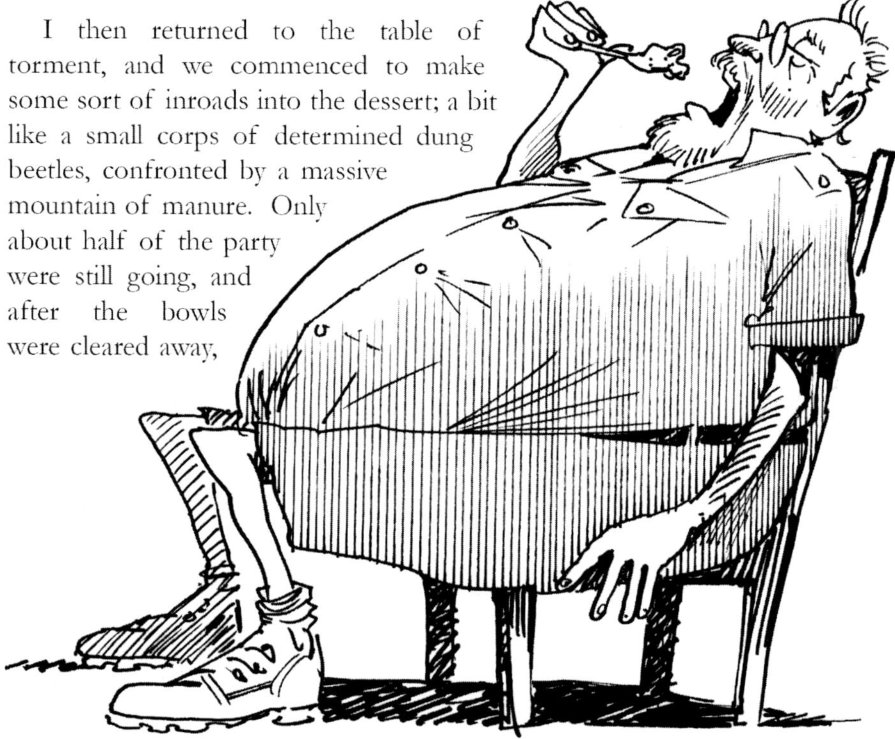

Ready to Burst

those left in the fray sat stunned, in shell-shocked silence, fearfully awaiting the next raid. Just as we were about to think that it was all over, two waitresses marched in carrying cheese and greens, on two very large wooden platters.

As they disappeared in the direction of the kitchen, others appeared bringing coffee, thus signalling the end of this extraordinary culinary epic.

A little while later, as we poked half heartedly at the platters, a young waitress whispered in my ear that the chef had a large package of frozen leftovers for me to take west. I nodded unbelievingly, and a short time later, I stood up again and walked past the truckies' table. I saw they were sitting like a couple of Black Kites, staring hopefully at the considerable quantities of cheese and greens that remained on our table. I made my way to the kitchen, and expressed my gratitude to the staff, but I couldn't find the manager. The chef loaded me up with a large polythene container, containing a mass of frozen barramundi, and prawns in dry ice, to take to the Continent's western extremity.

We said goodbye to the party, though some seemed incapable of answering. They were to catch a midnight coach to Perth, for which I didn't envy them at all. Patti, my mate Ian Fleiter and I, hopped in the OKA and headed west, intending to get a hundred kilometres or so under our belts before we camped. After about ten minutes of driving, it seemed like a real good idea to stop and roll out the swags, in amongst some bush, just off the highway.

I was still awake when I heard the sound of an approaching vehicle, and saw the coach glide past. I tensed myself in case there was an almighty explosion, like the restaurant scene from that famous Monty Python epic.

Footnote. I never did get to the bottom of that mystery dinner. On ringing the roadhouse, on our return journey home, I was informed that the roadhouse was under new management, and that the previous manager had left under somewhat unusual circumstances. I could understand that; the meal must have been worth in excess of $2000. It wasn't a bad dummy run.

24.

A Visitor From Outer Space

It was in the early 1990s and we were living at the Range, a bush block in the Mount Lofty Ranges, up behind McLaren Flat. Summer was well advanced, the time was around midnight, and my eldest daughter, Georgi and I, had just arrived back home from Adelaide. Georgi had gone to her room, and I was in our room, sitting on the end of our bed, getting undressed. I was down to my underpants when all of a sudden there was an ear-shattering ***Bang,*** which came from just outside the house. Georgi yelled out from downstairs that the Pink Gum tree in front of the house was all lit up. Thoughts raced through my head, seeking an explanation, but all I could imagine was this scenario.

There is a little oval and a hall, up on top of the range, about a kilometre from us, and this hall sometimes gets hired out to private groups for small functions. I thought that someone must have got on the grog, come down through the scrub, and shot some ducks on my dam. They must have then lit a quick fire to cook them. Sounded a bit far-fetched, but no other idea presented itself. Totally irrational, but I thought that they were maybe on drugs as well. Whichever way I looked at it, I didn't like it, but I had to do something about it. I dug out my .357 revolver, and clad only in a pair of underpants, crept in darkness down the stairs, telling Georgi to lay low, as I passed her room. The Pink Gum tree was indeed lit up, with a sort of unnatural light. As I let myself outside, I didn't exactly relish the thought of finding anyone, because considering their behaviour, they were probably off their faces, so a loaded revolver might not be the answer.

There was a railway sleeper retaining wall near the tree, and with some trepidation, I peered around the end of it. There was a campfire, but I saw with great relief, that there was no sign of anyone present; but this was no ordinary campfire. As I walked up to inspect it, I felt a lot of heat radiating from it, and it appeared the cherry red colour of Gidgee coals. I could then see that it wasn't wood burning, but molten metal. It suddenly hit me that we had almost been nailed by a meteorite, what else? I called Patti, Georgi and Kate down to have a look at it, and we studied the scene with great interest. It had landed on about the only bit of bare ground on the property, the bare clay of the dam bank, some three metres away from the water's edge. 'Lucky', I thought, 'anywhere else and it would have started a fire'.

It was very exciting, more so as I thought about the possibilities. When you push your own barrow, a bit of free publicity doesn't go amiss. Next morning I rang the newsrooms of various T.V. stations, as well as the *Advertiser*, reporting the events of the night before. I then phoned my mate, Bill Oliver, a farmer from near McLaren Vale, who sounded very interested, and drove up immediately to have a look, as did a few others that I rang. I mean, it's not every day that a meteorite lands in your back yard.

That morning, three TV stations, and the *Advertiser*, came out and were duly impressed. Looking for maximum impact, (no pun intended) I mentioned to one journo that it was lucky that it hadn't fallen a day earlier. "Why is that?" they asked. I replied, "Well, I had three camels tied up in that very spot." (A fact that was almost true). "You have camels here?" they asked; and so, of course, I took them over to my camel paddock, where the camels were duly filmed. 'All grist for the mill', I thought, and it certainly didn't do the story any harm, either.

I had earlier contacted the South Australian expert on foreign bodies, a professor at Flinders University. Strangely, he didn't think that it was of much importance, and as he was about to depart on an overseas trip, he was unable to come out. That evening though, a couple of very large gentlemen arrived from the U.F.O. Society (Unidentified foreign objects) to view the phenomenon, and were both quite impressed. They took many flash photographs, before returning to their vehicle, a small panel van, while I went back inside. Patti and I were watching TV, when about twenty minutes later, Patti remarked that there was a vehicle outside. I opened the door, and sure enough, there were the two large U.F.O blokes in their little van, making repeated unsuccessful attempts to drive up the steep gravel approach to our house. Diplomatically I suggested that one of them should sit in the back of the van, to give more traction to the rear wheels. They rearranged their seating, and their next attempt at negotiating the driveway was successful.

Over the next week or so, there were numerous phone calls from around the country, including a few calls from a bloke who lived on Horn Island, off the tip of Cape York Peninsula. He was a keen collector of meteorites, and kept telling me that I should, on no account, let the authorities convince me that it was not a meteorite. In fact, the opinion of various experts was that this was a thermite bomb, a device used by the railways workers to weld continuous lengths of railway line. My suspicions were now growing stronger, and I was beginning to think that I was a victim of a monumental practical joke, and the more I thought about it, the more it made sense. The first thing was that, if the device had landed anywhere else on the 58-acre property, apart from in one of the three dams, it probably would have started a fire. So it seemed quite a coincidence that it landed where it did, on the open clay area of the dam, no chance of a bushfire there. The other evidence was the expert university analysis of the samples that I sent them, their opinion being that it was, in fact, the result of a thermite bomb. It was quite a while before I extracted admissions of guilt from a couple of my mates, but we should let them give their version of the story.

Author's Note: The Other Side of the Story (Bill and Stoney's Version)

On the night in question Bill and Stoney had arrived up 'at the range' where I lived. They knew I was going to Adelaide that night, and had come prepared. They hid their vehicle and hid themselves in scrub until they saw Georgi and I drive off. A casual observer would have taken some interest in their appearance, they wore on their feet two huge sets of home made 'Kadaitcha Boots' (Australian Aborigines used these, made of emu down stuck together with blood, to carry out acts of revenge — they left no individual track and kept the wearer anonymous) constructed from hessian. They knew I was used to noticing tracks and took no chances.

Stoney had a .303 rifle slung over his shoulder, while Bill had the Hematite 'bomb' material slung over his back. They lay hidden in the bush until Georgi and I arrived home and, giving us time to get into bed, crept slowly down the steep hillside to the dam, moving to the side nearest the house.

After setting up the device, they ignited it, waiting until it released its maximum brightness, before firing a round up in the air from the rifle under our bedroom window. Seconds later when the contents of the device

Visitor from Outer Space

Stoney and Bill in their 'Kadaicha' boots

had been reduced to a molten metal, they then removed themselves to scrub near the house and observed my 'antics'. After a good night's work, they returned to Bill's farm. Next morning Bill received my phone call and was first on the scene, full of wonder as to what had taken place!

It is probably appropriate here for me to apologise belatedly to the various media and others who attended the scene, believing a meteorite had indeed landed. I had to give it full marks in the practical jokes stakes — I came in 'hook line and sinker'.

25. The Buggered Bustard

It was in the late 1970s, and I was operating a four-wheel drive, ornithological safari across the Gibson and the Great Sandy Deserts, to the Kimberley. It involved six or seven days of very slow, low gear travelling, across one of the, severely washed out, Len Beadell tracks. So bad was it that, much of the time, we simply used it as a navigation line, driving along in the general direction.

One morning we spotted a bustard out in the spinifex, quite a common sight out in this area, but it appeared to have something wrong with it, as it was dragging one wing along the ground. It seemed quite possible that it might have been attacked by a Wedge-tailed Eagle, and suffered some injury. On a previous occasion, I have seen one of these eagles swoop on a large, flying bustard. Anyway, I jumped out of the International and started to run after the bird, and when it realised that it couldn't escape, it bailed up and turned to face me. I should mention here that I was wearing a pair of shorts at the time, so I was fairly vulnerable. As I leant forward to grab the large bird, it lunged towards me, its head darting forward and striking me on the pecker. That set me back for a moment, and those people in the trucks, observing the performance through binoculars, had a very good laugh. I eventually managed to seize the bird, holding both wings securely to its body, and carried it back to the vehicles.

We decided then to have an early lunch break, and to use the extra time to attend to the wounded bird; someone had named it Strad. One of the ladies produced a pair of panty hose, from which we fashioned a sling for Strad's damaged wing. We made a comfortable position for him in the back of one of the Internationals, alongside a drum of fuel, which meant that we could open up a flap of the canvas side, to allow him/her some fresh air. This situation was the cause of a small bureaucratic problem, which seemed to concern some of our members.

It is illegal to have in one's possession, without an appropriate permit, any protected Australian animal or bird. Around the campfire that night, the argument persisted for what, I thought, was an unreasonable length of time, so I simply said to them, "Here's the deal. We can put the bird back in the bush where a dingo could secure an easy meal, I can shoot it here and now or we can take it for a ride." The take it for a ride option was the unanimous decision.

Every morning, lunchtime and evening, one or other of the party would take Strad for a walk on a lead. He soon got the hang of this, and even managed to feed himself, to some extent, digging up caterpillars, grubs etc. While this was happening, other party members would collect food for him, including his favourite, centipedes. He actually started to put on a bit of condition, becoming quiet and calm in his mobile domestic situation. We were becoming quite attached to him, though I still had vivid memories of his brutal and incredibly efficient attack on my nether region.

We eventually arrived in Broome, civilization after our ten days out in the desert. I pulled up at a service station to refuel, forgetting all about Strad. As the bloke was filling up my offside tank, a sudden commotion started up as Strad let go one of his unusual noises; very difficult to describe. "What the hell's that?" exclaimed the attendant, and I said to him, "It's probably just air in one of my fuel drums", pretty unconvincing, but it seemed to satisfy him OK. When we stopped for our evening camp, we had Strad out

Pecked on the Pecker

for his constitutional, later tying him to a tree where he squatted down quite happily.

A few days before our safari arrived back in Adelaide, we noticed that Strad had developed a swelling on his left upper leg. It had been my intention to let him go, and to recuperate in my fox and cat-free fauna reserve at Douglas Scrub, but I decided that I should drop him off at the Adelaide Zoo, where David Schultze, a distant relation of mine, was the chief veterinarian. This story, I'm sad to say, does not have a happy ending. David rang me the following day to tell me that Strad had died, apparently of septicemia, caused by his injuries. This was a great pity after his big adventure, and all the dedicated work that the party had put in.

26.

The Limmenbight Big Fella

In the early eighties, I was operating a safari in the Top End, and we had three vehicles, with a party of fifteen people. We were heading south on the Roper Bar to Borroloola road, which was just a sandy wheel track at that time.

About mid afternoon, we came upon the Limmenbight River, so I pulled in and set up camp on the southern bank, a hundred metres upstream from the rocky crossing, which was dry, and two metres above water level.

Things have changed now, but then I always used to carry a gill net in the back of the truck. We took it out this day, and attaching one end to a nearby tree, two of us swam and waded across the river to run out the net. We tied it onto a tree on the north bank, and then swam back to the camp. Crocs were not on our minds, as they are not seen or heard about in the upper reaches of these tidal rivers at that time.

We were sitting down enjoying a beer before our evening meal when Bill, who had been fishing in the river, came back to the camp in some excited manner saying, "this river's running backwards." Just then, we began to hear the roar of the water as it came over the crossing, and the river in front of us changed dramatically. The water, which contained a lot of mud and debris, had taken over our beautiful blue waterhole. It's always a pretty good floor show when the incoming tide pushes all the fresh water back up river.

After about half an hour, we could see that the net had developed a large curve, and realised that it must have been full of fish. I decided to swim across to release the net, but had to end up cutting the rope on the other side. This allowed the net to drift across the river to where it settled on the camp side bank. I swam back across to our camp, and was amazed to see the number and the variety of fish in the net. There were mangrove jacks, catfish, small barramundi, a stingray, small sharks, up to a metre in length, and many more. We selected a metre-long swordfish, with a saw about 45 centimetres long, and then set about the sizeable task of releasing the net, which had many good size holes in it. We cut the swordfish up with a hacksaw, into thick, round, white steaks, and that night's dinner was one of the most enjoyable that I have ever had.

Next morning I called into Nathan River station, just down the track a little way. I would always offer a trade at cattle stations – a flagon of good McLaren Vale wine, for a sugar bag of steak – and I did so on this morning. I was having a yarn to the manager and the conversation went a bit like this. "Did you camp down at the crossing last night?" he asked, to which I replied, "Yes we did and we had a very good night." He asked, "Did you see the Big Fella?" I paused here, for a few moments of sober thought, before replying, "What big fella?" The manager said "There's a twelve foot salty living in the waterhole, on the downstream side of the crossing, as well as a sixteen footer on the upstream side." *That was where we were camped.* I digested that bit of information, while I contemplated my walking and swimming across the waterhole on the previous evening, and then again when the net was full of fish. "No we didn't see him" I responded, but my mind was preoccupied, as we drove on south to Borroloola.

Now, whenever I cross the Limmenbight, I give a bit of a shudder. It must have been my good fortune that the Big Fella must have been in between good feeds.

Note: Some years later when I was traversing this route, I arrived at the now concreted causeway across the Limmenbight. There was a Kombi van parked there, with two very excitable young Germans. The couple told us they had just seen this huge crocodile enter the river. We walked up the bank about one hundred metres, and sure enough, there was one of the biggest sets of croc tracks I had ever seen. All food for thought.

27.

Two Close Perishes

During my time spent in the bush, I can remember many occasions when I was pretty dried out. This is an account of two of these occasions, where I went fairly close to "doing a perish"; it is not to be recommended.

Simpson Desert

In 1970, a surveyor friend of mine contracted me for a six-week job in the Simpson Desert. He was doing a second order level survey, and required me to cart his water, as well as work in the survey team. At the time, I was using 4 x 4 two-ton internationals, converted into safari wagons. They were six seaters, with a big rear-loading area under canvas. The only down side I thought was that November and December were the months that we were to do it.

The surveyor, John, was to do this levels survey, from near the old Pedirka railway siding, to Dalhousie Springs, on the edge of the desert, then along the French Track to Poeppels Corner, the convergence of the S.A., N.T. and QLD State borders. The last section was along the S.A. / QLD border to the Birdsville Track. A second order levels survey, gives a system of levels between the bench marks that had earlier been established by National Mapping. This six weeks work was to make a good start before knocking off for the summer.

I met John in Adelaide and our little convoy headed north, on a very pleasant November morning. It consisted of three short wheelbase land rovers, and my International, full of water drums. Late on the first day, we called into the old Farina store, the only place inhabited at the time, in the ghost town of Farina. Farina was once pretty significant, with three pubs and other solid stone buildings. Its name is Latin for flour, and it used to be the Southern end of the Strzelecki Track. In the late 1800's, during ten exceptionally good years, there were farming towns surveyed, all the way to the N.T. border, but of course, the seasons reverted to normal, and this never happened.

John and Beth knew Mr. and Mrs. Bell, a very fine old couple, who still kept the Farina store, an exceptionally solid, stone building. Tragically, their son had been posted as missing during world war two, however they had never lost hope, expecting him to one day return. They had even kept his room ready for this occasion.

There was no power connected, so we sat in a darkened room, with light from a kerosene lamp, having a cup of tea and a yarn. Next day, after travelling up what is now called the Oodnadatta Track, we set up our first surveying camp, near the Pedirka railway siding. Heading out the following morning, we settled into a pattern of work that would be repeated every day, for the next six weeks. Roger, Russ and I would hold the large survey staffs, while John would take readings through the theodolite, and record them. We would then move on, shifting the Land Rover as we did so. The weather had turned particularly hot for this time of the year, most days hovering around 40 degrees.

The first couple of weeks, we worked our way across the small Pedirka Desert, rolling gibber plains, intersected by watercourses of picturesque Red Mulga trees. They really are red, particularly in the early mornings and late afternoons, and at certain times of the year, are poisonous to stock. They have a limited distribution, occurring mainly in northeastern South Australia, the "heart break corner" area of southwest Queensland, also in the country just off the western edge of the Gibson Desert. They made comfortable camps, with a bit of welcome shade.

Holding the staff still for minutes at a time, was particularly hot work, especially in the hours until late afternoon, but nevertheless I was quite enjoying it, most of the time my brain was in neutral. Gradually we came into the Dalhousie Mound Spring area, passing the ruins of the old Dalhousie Station with its date palms, planted by early Afghan cameleers. A good landmark, the Dalhousie area near the western edge of the Simpson Desert, is one of the most desolate looking areas in Australia. Even in a good season, the powdery, salty soil grows very little grass or herbage, just a few scraggly perennials. However, there is dramatic contrast supplied by the areas of green reed beds, and patches of dryland Ti tree that mark the various mound springs. The water temperatures are various shades of warm, and at the centre of the complex is Spring Hut, a little shed near the biggest open water lagoon. At this time, the springs were included in Rex and June Lowe's pastoral lease of Mount Dare station, but it is now a National Park. Annually they would host a fly in, where a large number of light aircraft would fly in, for a weekend of fun and festivities.

We made a welcome base camp here at the lagoon, where the water is many metres deep, and although warm, is still refreshing to swim in. We put in a few hours there. Two weeks after setting up our camp at Dalhousie, we moved to another camp, about five kilometres west of the huge claypan that is the Finke River flood out, and the boundary of the Simpson Desert. This particular day, we just knew was going to be a stinker. Normally, we would do three miles of surveying, then check the levels on the way back to the vehicle, before driving up to do the next three miles. It was about 11am by the time we finished the first three miles, with the temperature well into the forties. To everyone's surprise (dismay), John decided to do another three miles. I didn't like the idea, but he was the boss, so we got on with it.

It was a long three miles, taking us right out onto the shimmering bare claypan of the Finke. To the east, the red sand dunes of the Simpson Desert danced around in mirage. Without any words spoken, we turned straight away and began checking the levels; we were six miles from our vehicles. I was in my late twenties, and probably as fit as anyone, being used to summer contract fencing, but I was starting to feel faint and pretty wobbly. I noticed that Roger, a retired bank manager, tall fit and wiry, and of over sixty years, was literally staggering at times. No one was going to chuck in the towel first, so we staggered on in a sort of trance. I know that I had a raging thirst, you always keep off your water bottle for as long as possible in the mornings, because once you start, it's hard to knock it off. I was giving myself a couple of mouthfuls every twenty minutes or so, and only had less than quarter of my one litre bottle left, and knew that the others would be the same. All of a sudden, I heard someone croak something, and heard a staff drop to the iron hard claypan. As if governed by one mind, the four of us started shuffling towards a Dead Finish bush, the only plant visible, and some two hundred metres away. With the seriousness that is usually reserved for drunks, we concentrated on the miserable bush, as though it was our only salvation; and maybe it was. On reaching it, ignoring its considerable large thorny foliage, the lot of us simply speared into it. Its shade was pathetic, but at least it was something.

The time now was around 2pm, and we lay in this bush until after 4pm, time that passed like a bad dream. I put my hat and handkerchief up above me, to throw shade on my face, but I could feel my tongue swelling, and I knew that wasn't a good sign. Every now and then, I would dribble a little water onto it, dreading the thought of emptying my bottle, and everyone else felt much the same. No one had spoken a word, because it was too bloody hard. I remember a bearded dragon crawling past my head, and propping himself up further in the bush, like the little sun worshipper that he was, and later a small flock of zebra finches, gaping bills indicating their stress, hopped around inches from my face. I'm sure that, if I had water to offer, they would have drunk from my hand.

When a little of the heat had gone out of the day, it was agreed that John and I would walk the four and half miles back to the vehicle, and return for the others. We set off, finishing the last of my water as I did so. Physically, that was one of the most difficult things I have ever done. My tongue felt like some foreign growth in my mouth, and I tried to put all of my limited concentration into not missing the next benchmark, a cross of whitewashed stones, with a star picket in the middle. If we were to miss it, the results didn't bear thinking about. We seemed to float along like zombies, until finally, after what seemed like an eternity, the Land Rover bobbed and wobbled in mirage, and we finally reached it. We weren't in good shape, so we dragged a two gallon polythene container full of hot water from the Rover, and collapsed on the shady side of the vehicle, backs to the wheels. It took all my will not to drink the bottle dry, but just to dribble the hot water gradually into my mouth; we each tipped some over our heads, which helped heaps. After around twenty minutes of trying to recover some energy, we crawled into the Rover, and drove back to the Dead Finish bush. The boys didn't look good, and Roger didn't seem to realise that we had returned. We helped them with the water, then drove very steadily back to our camp, which was a sick and sorry camp that night. I know I just managed to get down a few tinned peaches, but just had a craving for cold drinks. I probably would have given away five years of my life for a big cold frosty pint (bucket!) of beer. I didn't seem to sleep that night, spending much of it, sucking away at my water bottle.

All the next day, we dug out some sand from under the vehicle, and lay around dozing, drinking, and eating bits and pieces. At one stage, a mob of wild camels drifted through the camp, seeming to take great interest in us. I didn't know then, but these animals, or relations thereof, were going to play a big part in my life during the years to come, and they still are.

Next day we had all recuperated reasonably well, and had moved camp into the actual Simpson Desert. For nearly a week, we were on a clay track, but on reaching the Mokari turn off, we were suddenly into an occasional set of wheel tracks in the sand. Our tyres were let down to very low pressures, in order to get over the hot sand. The sand dunes have a steeper eastern face, and I had a few concerns about returning later on. For this job I had put on special Michelin, Sahara pattern, sand tyres, and thus began a love affair with this tyre, that lasted for many years.

The days passed, with the temperature rarely dropping below 38°, day or night, and all of our minds had a local picture of Utopia firmly entrenched, which was the Oodnadatta Pub. On one occasion, I offered to piggyback

John up a large sandhill, gear and all, for a carton of beer. He agreed to this, and I actually managed it (and duly collected my prize).

Finally, we came to the end of the survey, and started on the thirty odd miles through the dunes, back to the Mokari turnoff. We soon found that it was impossible to get up the eastern face of the hill, unless it was in the early hours of the morning. This we did, but soon came to a particularly steep, 70-foot dune that stopped us; no way could we get over it. We then put in a lot of time, digging a diagonal ramp with shovels, getting down to firmer sand. The ramp had to be wide enough to take the bigger International, so that was a lot of backbreaking labour. We waited until daylight next day, when the Land Rovers went over easily, with still more reduction in tyre pressure. I then drove the Inter over, very mindful of the risk of capsizing. We had to do the same earthworks on two more dunes, so it took us nearly three days to travel that short distance. It was with great relief that we reached the clay track, and headed back to Spring Hut for a long awaited plunge into the lagoon. We were also badly in need of a wash, as water had been heavily rationed.

We drove on, eventually camping thirty miles north of Oodnadatta, when nature played a nasty trick on us. It turned on a strong south/westerly cool change, greatly endangering our carefully nurtured thirsts. We were really annoyed about it as we crawled into our swags.

Next morning we arrived in Oodnadatta, and had a yarn with a good friend of mine, the late Yaro Pecanec (Pec) and Mrs. Pec, but declined their offer of drinks of any kind. When the pub door opened at 10am, we nearly knocked the publican down. After a couple of cold schooners, which didn't touch the sides, we settled down to drinking butchers, 7 ounce glasses. It just shows how dehydrated you can get. I sat on that barstool all day, moving off it just once to visit the toilet. We were like camels, reconstituting themselves after coming out of a long dry. Apart from feeling a bit wobbly around midday, before having a counter lunch, the beer didn't appear to have much effect. The litmus test was given when we walked out to our vehicles at around 5pm. Oodnadatta was a training station for police cadets, so there were three or four cops outside. We hopped into our vehicles, and with great deliberation, drove out of town to where we camped, forty miles out on the Hawks Nest road. We had to go via Coober Pedy, as thunderstorms had dropped a lot of rain around, just south of Oodnadatta, so we wouldn't have got through. It was a pleasant camp, with a large mulga fire, steak and yet more beers; it had been a long day.

We arrived in Coober Pedy next afternoon, with the temperatures up over the ton again. An old childhood mate of mine, was one of the only two police constables in Coober Pedy at the time, so we left our vehicles in the police compound for safe keeping, while we went to the pub. Our thirsts had more or less returned to normal by now, and we headed back to our swags at about 9.30pm, looking forward to a good sleep. At about midnight, we were rudely awakened by Kingsley, my policeman friend, roaring through the compound gate. He came over to our swags, saying that he wanted to deputise us; I was still "ticking over" fairly well, so I thought it sounded like a bit of fun. It seemed that a Yugoslav bloke, who was well known to the police, had gone berserk at the pub, and had nearly killed another bloke. Kingsley (the other constable was away on leave) took the three of us in his Land Rover to a dugout, five minutes away. We followed him down some narrow stone stairs, and when I saw what was sitting on the bed, I instantly became as sober as a judge. The man in question was about 5'8" x 5'8" and clad only in a pair of black footy shorts.

Kingsley formally told him that he was under arrest and asked him if he would come quietly. I listened with great interest for his answer, which was a snarled "Get !#*++#!, Copper, come and get me." In a split second, and in the interest of my immediate survival, I decided that I would make myself solely responsible for one of his massive arms. Yeah, that would do me. Kingsley jumped in, managed to get him in a headlock, and I followed, latched on to his arm, and that's when my trouble began. It began with the arm acting like a jackhammer, and I went up and down with it, thinking that if I let it go, I'm dead. The other boys had hold of other appendages, and it was a bit like trying to yard up a greasy pig at a rural show. He was sweating profusely, and so were all of us. We steadily got him up the stairs and into the cage on the back of the Rover. Kingsley slammed the gate closed, and with this, the suspect flew at the mesh, looked me in the eyes and hissed, "Who are you - I remember your face - I get you down a dark alley one night." Well, that certainly gave me food for thought. We drove back to the station, but when Kingsley told him to get out of the cage and into a cell, he suddenly picked up a length of towing chain that Kingsley had inadvertently left there. Shaking that like a mob of maraccas, he once again invited us to "come and get him." Shaking his head, Kingsley went into his quarters, reappearing in a pair of khaki combination overalls. He said it was to keep the blood off his uniform. I thought, "Well, bugger this," and picked up a decent lump of rock. I was fast coming to the conclusion that walking over sand hills is a bloody sight easier way to make a living.

There was one lone occupant of the lock up, an Aboriginal bloke, who was taking on the appearance of a beetle in a pit, with a scorpion about to join him. Kingsley got him to hold a powerful torch in the suspect's eyes, but the light soon resembled a Morse code session as the Aborigine squawked, "You're not gunna put that mad bastard in here with me are you boss?" The suspect was well known in the town. Then, all of a sudden, he threw down the chain, and walked out and into the cell, like a public servant heading for the loo. That was that, back to Kingsley's for a nerve-settling coffee, and once more to the swag. Those two constables had a big job to do in Coober Pedy, before they put a Sergeant up there and increased the manpower.

After another day in Coober Pedy, when we had to give evidence in court, we headed east to William Creek, and down to Marree. Here we heard that there'd been a cyclonic squall through Farina, destroying Bell's store. On arriving there the following day, an amazing sight met our eyes. Apart from a couple of walls left standing, the store was completely wrecked. Yet, hardly any other buildings had been touched. By a great stroke of good fortune (or fate), Mr. and Mrs. Bell had been on one of their rare visits to Adelaide, and were absent when it hit; all a bit hard to stack up and put away. They never returned.

Lake Everard (the Bronzewing Factor)

In 1962, I was jackerooing on Lake Everard, a two and a half thousand square mile sheep station, eighty miles south of Kingoonya, in northwest South Australia. There were two of us jackeroos on Childara outstation, near the dog fence, on the southeastern end of the Great Victoria Desert. We had a very interesting and carefree existence here, pretty much our own bosses. Once a week we would get a scratchy set of orders along the fencing wire phone line, that led 40 kilometres to the Lake Everard homestead. A little bit of horse work, but mostly we used big, ex army, 750cc Harley Davidson motorbikes, for mustering. We also had a long wheelbase station Land Rover. Part of our job was to do a monthly run along the dingo proof fence, along a track that had the highest dunes, along the world's longest fence.

One day, we had orders to muster Peninsula paddock. Now Peninsula was no ordinary paddock, it was 130 square miles of sand dunes, small saltpans, with thick Mulga, Black Oak and Native Pine bush, and had been previously fenced off from the rest of the station, because of a lack of water. The northern part tucked itself up into the southern end of the 500 square mile salt Lake Everard. It was actually a great slice of wilderness and we looked forward to going out there. We packed about three days stores in the Land Rover, and loaded one bike in the back with the other gear. I rode the other bike out to a tank and yards called Hopkins, where we set up a camp. Some months back, a mob of wethers had been put out there, and we had to check to see if they were watering OK, at the only water point, Hopkins tank. The danger was of them getting out and feeding on a succulent called Parakeelya, where they wouldn't require water. When the Parakeelya eventually dries up, they can perish, being too far to walk back to water.

We took our lunches and half a gallon of water each to drink, and to boil our quart pots at lunchtime, and we each headed off in separate directions. Neither of us knew this paddock, so we didn't make any arrangements to meet for lunch. It was November, the temperature was in the mid thirties, and I had an enjoyable morning, seeing some interesting country, and thinking that this wasn't a bad way to make a crust. I saw a couple of hundred sheep, all full of water, and couldn't see any sign of Parakeelya, which is a small plant like Pigface, but on average, as big as your hand, with a purple flower. I had lunch, and boiled my quart under a big Native Pine, on top of a sand hill, and after lunch, I began working back towards where I reckoned Hopkins tank was. At about four o'clock, I rode through some dead sticks, and got a piece of Mulga jammed between the chain and the sprocket, bringing me to a sudden halt. Try as I did, there was no way I could get that stick out, only having a pocket knife and small tyre lever with which to try. After an hour, and a lot of sweat, I gave it away. Nearly all my water was gone, and to be honest, I wasn't too sure exactly which way Hopkins was. If I had been mobile, I would have hit one of the two fences, or one of the sheep pads, heading towards the water, but I wasn't. The more I thought about it, the more serious I realized my predicament was. I only had another two hours of daylight, and could only travel until dark, there being no moon. If I headed in the wrong direction, my real trouble would start next morning, after a night without water. I knew how to get water off the roots of some trees, but I would need a machete or similar, and you generally use up as much fluid getting it out as what you get out of it. I began walking, heading in the direction where I thought the Hopkins tank was about half an hour after the sun set.

A Bronzewing pigeon flew past me, straight as a die, in a southwesterly direction. I have always been a birdman, and I knew that bronzewings would always fly uninterrupted, direct to water, whereas once they have watered, they do a bit of feeding on their way out to roost in the evenings.

I thought to myself that I had better have the courage of my convictions, and taking a rough bearing, I headed off in the direction taken by the pigeon. This was about 15° different to the course I was taking. After about an hour of walking, I came across a fresh sheep pad, and twenty minutes later, I saw the tank through the mulga, a beautiful sight. My mate had a hurricane lantern tied to the top of a tree and the billy boiling, realizing I was in trouble, and I had an interesting tale to tell. There are many different birds that I am fond of, but the bronzewing has a very special place in my heart. I'll probably never know how much I really owe that bird.

28.

Sea of Sand Dunes

In 1988, I decided to operate a really major camel expedition in the Great Victoria Desert. Over the years I had organised six others, ranging from 14 to 24 days, some of them filling in a few blank spots on the map. This one would be mainly in South Australia, but included a few days in Western Australia.

In May of 1999, I had a 14-day ornithological camel safari organised, beginning at Ooldea on the transcontinental railway. This is also literally the border between the eastern end of the Nullarbor Plain, and the Great Victoria Desert. This would help to make the main expedition more viable. At the same time, Outback Camel Company's operations were happening, in and around the Simpson Desert. My partner, Andrew Harper, was looking after that.

Even though we are well used to mounting expeditions, there is always an enormous amount of work involved. There would be even more if I pandered to the whims of every bureaucracy supposedly involved. In fact, if I did everything that the shiny bums dictated, these trips would never happen. I subscribe to the theory that, if you water a weed it grows. Bureaucracy is like that. I am not an unreasonable person. Many laws are made for the betterment of man and the environment, and therefore quite necessary. I have common sense, reasonable intelligence, and believe in the word 'sustainability'. I know that what I am doing is generally worthwhile. It gives me a tenuous dollar, the camels a walk and feed, my clients a lot of pleasure, and sometimes adds to science. Therefore, let no shiny bum stand in the way of all these worthwhile things.

So it was that in early June, 1999, I am driving with an OKA-load of cameleers and party members, on the Eyre Highway. That evening we pull into the home of a mate called Spitta, who lives in the low bush at the back of the Great Australian Bight, 20 kilometres south of the little town of Penong;

a comfortable shed home, with only metres away, an incredible, partly-built, hexagonal, two storey home, built of Hebel bricks, rising above the Ti-tree.

His wife, Trina, and his children, live a good bush life here. Spitta has his own camels, and because of the two operations going at once, my resources are stretched. I am hiring Spitta, and five of his camels as well. He is not present as he is running the shorter ornithological trek with a mutual mate, Johnny Whittaker. My wife, Patti is with me for the first 21-day section of the 43-day expedition.

Party members include Stavros Pippos, a well known landscape photographer, Toddy Bailey, from the Adelaide Hills, Pat Coen likewise, Richard and Pat Duncan from the same area, and Michael Rainsbury, an Englishman who had done a few other big trips with us. Also, Maria Visconti, a journalist doing a story on the expedition. Other cameleers were Jason Downs and Darren Hassan.

Next morning we headed off early, Trina and the kids following us in their 4WD ute, meeting Spitta, their husband and father on the changeover. We drove along the highway, past the Nullarbor Roadhouse, to the turnoff that led north across the open Nullarbor Plain to the little outpost of Cook, on the transcontinental line. The Nullarbor is the biggest limestone plain in the world, covered for the most part, by the long-lived Bluebush, a low tough blue/grey shrub; a boring desolate place to most of the population, but a fascinating addictive region to those who know it. My years on developing stations on the western side of the Nullarbor were some of the best I have spent.

We duly arrived in Cook, where a local caretaker bloke fixed me up with three 44-gallon drums of water. Then came the tricky little task of locating the camel camp. With an extra large party, they had not been able to make the arranged rendezvous at the Cook – Vokes Hill Track, and were some fifty kilometres short, in a donga. (A donga is a depression in the plain into which, lots of topsoil has been washed, over many years. Most have a variety of trees and shrubs, usually Black Oak, Mulga, Myoporum and Bullockbush, or sometimes just the one species. They are like islands in a sea of grass or Bluebush). With the aid of a GPS, and using a network of old rabbit trappers' tracks, we finally located the camp, a couple of hours before dusk.

Changeovers at camel camps are very confusing affairs. One group, having done the trek, are laid back and relaxed, while the incoming group is usually in various degrees of being hyped up, concerned, excited or a mixture of all three. There is a shocking conglomeration of gear, camels, saddles, pack bags, etc. Socially they are not an ideal situation. The outgoing group usually harbours something that borders on resentment towards the new group. Total isolation has that effect on the normally most sociable of people.

Next morning there is more chaos, until finally the vehicles take away the outgoing crew, and a sort of peace reigns. Mountains of stores are stowed in canvas pack bags and large timber, and in this case steel, boxes. The outgoing crew were delayed for an extra hour, because Johnny Whittaker decided to give us an extra hand with loading up, something that he is very good at. We had lunch, and finally jumped up the string of 16 camels, and staggered off on our thousand-kilometre odyssey. On the first day, almost any distance travelled is a bonus, although I am never really happy unless I get at least eight or ten kilometres under the belt.

If a load does not fall off in the first ten minutes, you know you've done something right, so you begin to relax, and look forward to the day's walk. It's a bit like working a dairy farm. You do your work in the morning and the late afternoon, and not much through the day.

We were travelling across the northern part of the Nullarbor Plain, limestone country, but the further you get from the centre of the plain, the softer the country gets, as the soil has a greater depth. There are a lot more dongas, and selecting one of these, about an hour and a half before sunset, I hooshed the string down, after having done about six kilometres. It was a start, anyway. Unloading beats the hell out of loading up. While some of the party hobble the camels, we organise others to take off swags, pack bags, top bags and the big boxes, until you have a line of humps with just the saddles on.

At this stage, we perform a nasty little con trick. You have to start taking saddles off from the rear, moving towards the front. If you remove the front saddle, it's on the cards that the camel will get straight up. This can then precipitate the rising, en masse, of the rest of the string, with their saddles still on; something you wouldn't want to know about. A long time ago, I worked out a system that works really well. We go along forwards, from the rear, taking off the cruppers, girths, and breastplates, leaving the saddles on the camels. The camels still stay hooshed (mostly!), then you get a couple of crews organised to whip off the saddles. The saddle-less camels begin to stand up, but the front camels with saddles still on are down. You have a couple of 'stringers' floating around, ready to tug on a camel's lead rope and yell, "Hoosh", if any try to stand up with their saddles on. The saddles are off in a short time, placed next to the camel's position with that saddle's loads next to it, either side. Now it's 'playtime' for the camels. They look around, and being good botanists, identify the best available camel tucker and shuffle off in their hobbles in that direction. This afternoon, there are still two camels hooshed down, both with their necks and heads stretched out, like lizards drinking. They are the big bullocks, Chaluk, and his younger colleague, Jacky Jack. Both these camels demand a vigorous scratch behind the ears from someone before they get up. It's a very endearing trait from such large animals; gentle giants.

The humps are out browsing and grazing, and in bush country, we organize 'shepherds' to keep an eye on them. It's easy to lose individual camels in thick scrub, and valuable time (especially in the mornings) can be lost in tracking them down. It's a relaxing time for party members, being around the camels when they are totally relaxed and 'knocked off'. They like to wallow in mud, water, dirt or sand, and on occasions, you might see a camel, enjoying a wallow with up to half a dozen waiting their turn. Every time the wallow is used, it becomes a better proposition. As camels browse, they move from here to there, their mobile rubbery lips nibbling off vegetation, rarely taking the lot, unless it happens to be Quandong or some Mistletoe, their favourites. It is not a pretty sight to see a Quandong tree, reduced to a sticky looking skeleton in a matter of minutes, by hungry camels. Sometimes you get the whole string radiating around a feed tree, like spokes of a wheel, and that makes a great photograph, with their long narrow backsides, and flying tails pointing outwards.

When dusk approaches, we go around and tie the camels to individual feed trees, making sure there is no chance of them becoming tangled during the night. In the early days, when a lot of our camels were half wild, we would often have to jump out of our swags through the night, to attend to tangled up camels. Sometimes, with only torchlight, it seemed impossible to sort out, and on many occasions, a swift kick in the guts would do the trick. They would spring up, becoming disentangled in the process, but not always. Sometimes we would even have to cut ropes, something we hated doing. In this business, you need to have a dying grandmother, who owns a rope factory. Every night the pattern is much the same. The fire is lit and the cooks get busy. The hors d'oeuvres are put out; usually dry biscuits and dip, while it lasts. After that we generally serve smoked oysters, cheese or similar.

The first night is always different, as people get used to the set up. Some take their swags some hundreds of metres away, while others camp not far from the fire. I always have a policy of not letting them camp too close. Staff are up and about before daylight, and you do not want to be treading on heads. On this occasion, I noticed that a couple had set up a small bright flashing red light by their camp on a low rise; must be to help them find their way back to camp in the dark. You see some things.

Next morning we were off at a more respectable hour, around quarter to ten. Makes a huge difference, having each camel's load in place, and the crew beginning to get a glimmer of what is happening. And speaking of glimmers, here's a funny one for you. Richard and Pat, the couple with the flashing red strobe light, forgot to get it when they packed up; it wasn't obvious in the daylight. Consider this: That bright little light will be operating for around the next umpteen years, without a pause. Makes you wonder how the local wildlife will adjust to it.

The next couple of days, we gradually walked out of the northern Nullarbor, and into what is known as the 'Myall Belt'. It's a buffer zone between the Nullarbor and the Great Victoria Desert, comprised mainly of Bluebush and Myall trees. There is a scattering of Myoporum, Mallee, Mulga and Bullockbush, but nearly all the former.

Mid morning, we came across a patch of surface limestone, with what seemed like a couple of logs sticking out of it. On closer inspection, we saw that it was a blowhole, like that found extensively on the southern part of the Nullarbor. I am not sure if this was a 'blower' or not, as they only do that in the heat of the day, further south. It could be that a party of Aborigines had earlier put these logs of Myall in the hole for some reason, as they were very old. There were no signs of old wheel tracks since we started. Occasionally rabbit trappers and doggers would drive up into this country, looking for prospects. A few hundred metres on, we found a small cave in a patch of limestone, and a couple of us went down for a look. We went down about eight metres, on a couple of levels, with a number of old bones on the bottom. Some were rabbits; there was a dingo skull, and others we could not identify, so we put them in a plastic bag for delivery to the museum later on. Patti, my longhaired mate, was with me on this trip, so the meals took on a few extra degrees of sophistication.

We were about to pull up for lunch on the third day. Spitta was leading the string on foot and I was mounted on Sahib, looking for a likely lunch camp, when we sensed a 'rort'. It's just a feeling you get, and sure enough, there is a pounding of many feet and a rattling of loads, as the last two thirds of the string begin rushing forward. Spitta walked swiftly forward, and turned our leaders the opposite way to the 'tail' that was rushing forward, splayed out to the near side. All pulled up with no entanglement and all was well. There was a feral bull camel, somewhere to the rear, and this had caused the 'rort'. So we sat them all down, and put the billy on. No feral bull materialised, but the lunch was notable for the Thorny Devil that we found. These marvellous little bright brown and yellow lizards are always a welcome centre of attention when encountered. This one was hanging vertically from a dead Myall stump, and became the model for many photographs.

Later that day, a bull camel appeared out to our left, and was obviously in season. It was blowing white froth from the mouth, with the neck glands exuding that sticky dark fluid, and there were plenty of burbling sound effects. Spitta went out towards him, with his combination 12 gauge shotgun/. 222, under and over. After trying unsuccessfully to scare the bull off, he decided to shoot it. It never gives us any pleasure (quite the reverse) to shoot bulls, but it really is a 'them or us' situation. If they get among the string, particularly when loaded, we are in big trouble, and people's lives are at risk. It is one of the unfortunate legacies of travelling with female camels. We kept a good look out for more bulls around the camp that night, but as is often the case, this was an old lone bull.

On about the fourth day of the expedition, with some fifty-five kilometres travelled, we came across the first sand dunes of the Great Victoria Desert, and entered this massive and remarkable wilderness of sand and scrub, our second largest desert, next to the Great Sandy Desert further north. In my opinion, it is the most diverse and interesting of all our deserts.

One day around mid-morning we were walking along through open Blackoak and shrubland, when Stauros gave a shout. He was holding an object in his hands that turned out to be an old rusted water bottle. Obviously very old because metal objects take years to rust in deserts where there is no humidity. It turned out that we had travelled for a few kilometres on the route taken by explorer Richard Thelwall Maurice, on this 1902 expedition from Fowlers Bay on the Great Australian Bight to Cambridge Gulf on the Kimberley Coast.

The next few days, we travelled in a northwesterly direction, crossing the fifteen to twenty metre dunes obliquely, without much trouble. There was no need to split the string, as there sometimes is with large dunes. Usually Spitta or I would walk ahead, and pick the best route through the scrub on the dune. We were also having to avoid the camel poison bush, Gyrostemon Ramulosa, of which there was an increasing amount. I had never actually lost camels to this bush, but have had them sick and affected by it. Earnest Giles, the explorer, lost camels to this bush, on his west/east crossing of the Gibson Desert. It is not hard to identify, being a light green colour, with off-white coloured bark, and grows mostly on the sand hills. When mature, it can measure up to five metres in height. Mostly the camels look to browse it, so we have to position walkers near some bushes, to hunt the animals away as they move past it; always a worrying time.

The days slip by, and Spitta is worried about 'blowouts' appearing on the backs of some of his big bullocks. They carried very heavy loads on the previous trek, and coming into work in 'soft' condition (unworked for a long time), saddle sores were a very real possibility. There's nothing worse than saddle sores, when you have weeks of work ahead of you. They just don't get a chance to heal, and it means constant juggling of loads.

Some camels stand out as characters, and Sahib, my one-eyed, free-riding lead camel is special. Sometimes we would lead with him, other times I would free ride him, using him to scout country out on the wings. Sometimes other camels would pick on him, but it never seemed to bother him. Then there was Yellow Butt, a miserable beast that I was borrowing from Don Ainsbury, the cameleering cop. Everyone felt something between sympathy and disgust for Yellow Butt. He moaned whenever you went near him, and if pressed, would attempt to cover you in green stinking slime, with a cunning little flick of the head. He hated his life, was losing condition, yet would not eat when it was available. So what do you do with him? I saw him a year later, in his paddock back at Hallet, in South Australia's mid north. He actually had a good hump, and his body language seemed to indicate that he felt OK about himself.

A big favourite was Little Crow, one camel that I had recently purchased. A dubious bit of camel trading took place, when I went to pick up two large bullocks from a particular camel man. It was only two days before departure, and I found two babies yarded and ready so I had to take them, no option. It meant that they had to do work that was too heavy for them, on the ornithological trek, and saddle sores resulted. We actually had to truck Possum out before our trip and could not possibly work him; but Little Crow was not quite so bad. He had an enormous scab over a sore on his back, a sore that needed many changes of dressings. Spitta did a particularly good job on this, fancying himself as an amateur vet. Luckily, his small riding saddle could be fitted, and this just missed his wound, so it gradually improved. Crow has a great nature and I have high hopes for him. My old mate, Chaluk, was the tail end Charlie, near retirement from the big expeditions, as was his colleague, Raj). He just cruised along at the rear, carrying a couple of water canteens, a swag and a rider. You could sit back there on your riding period, and travel along in splendid isolation. Spitta's big bullocks were greatly admired, and his young camel, Streaky, was full of tricks, and was a bit of a pet.

One day we arrived at one of our early destinations, something that was marked as a claypan on the map. It turned out to be a very interesting feature, a bare claypan of around 500 acres, with a gypsum ridge on two sides, to the north and east. The eastern ridge had a smaller 'copi' (a powdered gypsum ridge) in front of it, that provided a good camp. We sat the camels down along its half-round top, under a patch of Black Oaks, *Casuarina cristata*, a species often associated with copi country. We camped at around 2.30pm, so had most of the afternoon to explore the area. However, before much else happened, a bull camel came steaming across the lake, heading for our feeding animals. Spitta went down and shot it, and this time we cut some steaks off.

I walked across the claypan, and climbed up on to the northern ridge. I found considerable signs of Aboriginal activity, mostly tules (scrapers) and tule slugs (the worn out remains of the same). Also a couple of reasonable hammer, or top grinding stones, showing that Aborigines used the area. The camels had located a few gallons of muddy water, and had soon sucked it dry. They did not need it, but will always top up the tanks, if an opportunity presents itself. Bird life was good, with the change in habitat. Saw a pair of red-capped robins, and grey shrike-thrushes were calling everywhere. A little falcon (Australian Hobby) had been seen skimming over the claypan, plus a pair of wedge-tailed eagles. The camel steaks turned out to be tender for a change, and Patti's excellent salad made the meal one to be remembered. This being a camel expedition, our food had to be washed down with a pannikin of port instead of a glass of red. We carry two 20-litre jerry cans of port, either side of the packsaddle, allowing for a pannikin a night each, which just fills the spot nicely.

More nor-westering, until we came across a broad watercourse that was the drainout of the Serpentine Lake System. We then dispensed with our compass navigating and followed it north along, or adjacent to, the western shoreline. The Serpentine Salt-lakes straddle the SA/WA border, and are definitely one of my favourite salt lake systems. From both ends, they start off in undramatic fashion, but about halfway along the approximately 150 kilometre long system, there are what can only be described as quite spectacular land forms. We came across one of these, a few days later, a four-metre high clay/gypsum cliff, with a big yellow-coloured, live sand dune on top. A couple of little mulgas provided some sparse change. Here the salt was a glistening white, and around a kilometre across. Lunch was had here, before moving on to a nice camp under big Black Oaks, on the other side of the lake. It was OK to cross here, but extreme care must be taken. Once bogged, it can be almost impossible to extricate camels, from the bottomless black ooze that lies under the salt crust. The camels walked a couple of kilometres south down the lake, on both sides looking for ground feed, and our shepherding took a fair bit of time today. We ended up tying up some of them, half a kilometre from camp; not ideal when feral camels are around. Bulls can kill bullocks, and when cows are in season, they can run away with feral bulls, even with hobbles on.

About mid way through the next afternoon, we came across what would be described in the USA as a box canyon. It ran at a right angle to the lakes, off to the west. We followed it in, with the string looking very photogenic, walking alongside a low cliff on its southern side. I went ahead on Sahib and found an excellent campsite, open ground with shade trees, backed by a twenty-metre cliff, with heaps of camel feed. It had everything but water, and I intended camping here for two nights. This 42-day expedition was split into two segments, and we were about two thirds of the way through the first. Everyone always appreciates a base camp, after a couple of weeks of non-stop trekking. Next day was a combination of lying around reading, and exploring the area, both on foot and by camel. I rode around, checking small caves in the breakaway for wildlife, in particular ghost bats. No luck here, but I have seen them a few times. This is our biggest bat (excluding flying foxes) and one of our most rare, and has a wingspan of around 50cm. No luck, but I did flush a barn owl, and added a few more birds to our list. Stavros Pippos went about his business here, of securing first-class photographs of the South Australian landscape. Well known for his photographic record of the Flinders Ranges, he was getting the last few records together, before publishing a large book on the whole South Australian landscape. Stavros strives for perfection in his photographs, sometimes only taking several in the course of a few days. In this case, he had his tripod set up at the entrance to our canyon, looking out across a varied botanical foreground along the length of the meandering lake. A lot of cloud made it difficult, but next morning, a few minutes of sunlight through the cloud, gave him the opportunity he was after. That photograph will appear in his book, *The Shades of Ochre*, published in 2001. After this trip, he accompanied me on several boat expeditions down the Diamantina River to Goyder's Lagoon Swamp and down the Warburton and Kallakoopah Rivers to Lake Eye. So impressed with this pictorial record of the South Australian environment, was the South Australian Government, that they are using this book as their official 'Giveaway' to visiting dignitaries.

After our well-deserved spell, we moved on through often-difficult terrain of jumbled dunes and thick scrub. On this trip we saw only three dingoes; they seem wilder here than in the more open deserts. There are plenty here, but they use the cover to their advantage. We did put up a species of kangaroo rat on two occasions; a huge flurry of movement and they were gone, with little chance of identification. On another lunch camp near the salt lake, Stubbie put up some kangaroo mice. We caught a couple, photographing them before letting them go.

One day, as we were about to cross to an easier situation on the east side, we came across a remarkable series of brown and white, half round rocks, covering about a quarter of an acre. They looked good enough to eat, and were quite soft, probably a type of mudstone. I had never before encountered anything like them. We crossed a narrow part of the lake without incident, heading towards a rocky bluff, some 30 metres high, on the eastern edge of the lake. Plenty of coloured stones here, including Agates. A couple of kilometres of excellent travelling, north along the eastern shore before encountering a system of narrow salt creeks, leading into a small flat, backed by dunes. A very good campsite with Pigface providing the main camel feed. With this succulent, like Munyeroo and Parakeelya, the camels literally 'leak like sieves'. It's as good as a drink of water.

It was here that something remarkable occurred. I was out tying up the last camels, just after sundown, and as I was wandering back towards the welcoming glow of our campfire, I was suddenly aware of literally dozens of birds flying low over my head toward the centre of the flat. I soon identified them as Bronzewing pigeons. Many birds, including pigeons, doves, and most parrots; most of the seedeaters in fact, require water twice a day. A couple of parrot species, in particular Scarlet-chested Parrots, have a talent where they can survive on the often-limited dew available. Budgerigars can bring up broods every six weeks, living only on green spinifex seed, without water. I am certain that Zebra Finches are similar. Blue Bonnets and Princess Parrots can survive well without physically drinking every day. Pigeons however, need to suck in some water twice a day, which was why tonight's little floor show was exciting me so much. The Bronzewings just kept coming, now in their hundreds. It was too dark to see where they were landing, but 1 quickly walked to the camp with this news. We are always looking for Night Parrots, having rediscovered them on Cooper Creek in 1979 (See my first book, *Bush Safari*). The samphire/spinifex country is classic habitat for them, only needing a reliable water source to top it off. Throughout the trip, we had been beating certain, well-vegetated flats, ably assisted by Stubbie, my active little Jack Russell terrier.

Next morning we found where the Bronzewings had been watering, and it was a very welcome discovery. There was actually, what must be a freshwater spring, located in the saltwater creeks. We would never have realised it had it not been for those flights of Bronzewings the previous night. The water was brackish, but certainly drinkable. A couple of us had a head wash on the way out with the camels, beating the flat as we went. No Night Parrots, but this wasn't the end of it.

The next camp, some seventeen kilometres to the NNW, was on some high ground, overlooking a sort of backwater of the lake. That night, as we ate, I heard the call of a night bird that was totally unfamiliar to me. It moved away before we were able to tape it, but I was convinced it was a Night Parrot; I know my desert birdcalls pretty well. There are limited night calls, and this one corresponded favourably with the Night Parrot's call, described in Simpson and Day's, *Birds of Australia.* Next day there was no sight of the bird but I resolved then and there, to mount another expedition here, and to spend at least a couple of days here with mist nets. The fact of the probably permanent freshwater source at the previous camp, established in my mind their presence here.

A few days later, we cut the Ann Beadell Highway, and moved a couple of kilometres north, out of sight of any four wheel drive traffic. Twenty-four hours were spent here while my OKA came in, bringing with it, almost a new party, including new cameleer, Luke Talbot-Male. There were Darren and Fiona Wallace, Brenton Hicks, and Brenton's 11-year-old son, Tom. Maria Visconti stayed, and her husband Simon came in, while Patti unfortunately, had to go home to keep my office running. Toddy Bailey and Pat Coen and the Duncans went out, as well as cameleer, Jason Downs. All very confusing to the reader, but we ended up with the same number of people, to continue on the second half of the expedition. This section would require an average of 22 kilometres a day, in order to get to our rendezvous with Roger and his transport. The camels were going well, and so far had no other saddle sores, with Little Crow now carrying a rider on some stages. Once again, we went through the irksome task of getting 23 days of water and stores packed in. We had enough to give the camels a few gallons each, and I'm sure they appreciated that.

After an early lunch, we headed off into jumbled sand dunes, which is often the case around the salt lakes. To some extent, we could plot our course through the area of least sand dune activity, provided it did not deviate from our route too much.

Later that afternoon, Darren put up a pair of Scarlet-chested Parrots, that exquisite little parrot whose stronghold is the Great Victoria Desert. I remember well my first experience of this bird. On a very hot February day, I was having lunch with my old mate, Two-Mile Sheedy, north of Neale Junction, further west in this desert. We were dumping a 44 gallon drum of petrol after a couple of months fencing, down on the Nullarbor. It was to be used on my 4WD safaris, later that year. The drum was bright silver, and was sitting at the base of the 15 metre Marbled Gum (*Eucalyptus gongilyacarpa*) that we were camped under. Suddenly this small parrot, the size of a plump Budgerigar, but with a longer tail, was hanging in front of us, seemingly attracted by the silver drum. Perhaps mistakenly perceived as a water source; much the same as ducks are attracted to an iron homestead roof on a moonlit night. What stood out was the brilliant scarlet chest, (in our faces) sort of thing. It fluttered away in confusion and the moment was lost but never forgotten, one of my favourite 'bird experiences'. I knew straight away that I had my first sighting of Scarlet-chests, and they have been a favourite ever since.

As we travelled, everyone was saddened to see the ongoing damage caused by rabbits. It appeared that the Calici virus had not jumped the buffer area between the Nullarbor and this central region of the Great Victoria Desert. I made a note to let the relevant authorities know, so that they could rectify this, hopefully. Stubbie was pretty happy about the situation, running lots of extra kilometres a day, in his constant quest to catch a rabbit. Jack Russells will kill them down a hole, but few dogs will actually catch a rabbit on the run. Every night he would lay down at the side of my swag, legs in the air, totally buggered. What a life he had!

A week passes and we are achieving our average, getting down to a lean mean travelling machine. I've got a new cameleer (Luke) who does not stop talking, but is the best potential cameleer material that I have had in years. We are travelling up this flat with low scrub when Stubble gives a yelp, and a rabbit jumps up under the lead camel's feet. Suddenly the sun is momentarily blocked out, as a Wedge-tailed eagle dives out of nowhere. I am on the front camel, and as my camera comes up, my camel goes briefly behind a bush. Just as the eagle is about to pluck the rabbit from the ground, six metres in front of me, it dodges and spurts away, scratching sand towards the sandhills. One of the walkers up there witnessed the Wedgetail clumsily flapping after the rabbit, but he had missed his chance; they often miss intended prey. I've always taken great interest in Wedge-tailed Eagles, and have been privy to many exciting little dramas. On two occasions, I have seen a single bird; drop large sticks on to a kangaroo, sheltering under a Mulga tree, with a good degree of accuracy. Some of the sticks hit their mark, from around twenty or thirty metres up, and on both occasions the 'blue flyer' (female Red Kangaroo) moved out into the open. On the first occasion, the pair of eagles would take it in turns to attack, riding the neck, and slashing the head viciously with their lethal bills, all the time buffeting them with massive wings. It was an example of how cruel nature can be. The 'flyer' wasn't exactly a flyer any more, barely able to hop. Eventually she just propped, and tried to face her attackers; with her head a bloody mess. I was on horseback at the time, and it was all I could do to prevent myself from galloping up to save the 'roo, but something prevented me from doing this.

After about half an hour, the 'roo was on her side, and was good as dead. The eagles were feeding and the crows were gathering; Just one of nature's floorshows. The second occasion was similar, but with just the one eagle, and it was going to take longer. I was on a motorbike mustering, with a mob of sheep in hand. I left them following along about a hundred metres behind. A fence interceded; the roo scrambled through the fence and seemed to be heading for a patch of Black Oak, over a kilometre distant. My sheep had buggered off, and my kelpie was frantically trying to hold them, so I reluctantly left the roo to its fate.

On two other occasions, I have seen eagles training their young to stoop and dive on prey. Both times, it was using a snake about a metre long. The parent would drop the snake and dive, catching it before it hit the ground. It did this several times, before giving the eaglet a go. The young bloke was so clumsy, that it almost went into the ground without catching the snake. It had three attempts, improving steadily, but I didn't see it catch the snake before they disappeared from view..

A regular traveller/mate of mine, Brenton Hicks, always makes my day. A successful Adelaide businessman, with a deep love and enthusiasm for the bush, and this was the second time he had brought along one of his boys. The first few days, Hicksy is staggering along, up the flats and over the dunes, sporting a huge pack, as well as his heavy calibre rifle; used to shoot the odd problem bull. He is sweating a great deal, and is drinking too much of our precious water. Alongside him is young Tom, with his smaller pack, energetically following his dad. I offer to stick Tom's pack on the camel, but Brenton declines and I can see what he's about. Tom appreciates it too, but can't quite see the point, when there are camels that can carry them; without knowing the difference. Eventually Brenton concedes and lightens his load, drinks less water, and sort of agrees that 'when in Rome etc.'. Sanity prevails, and Tommy puts his excess energy into bouncing quandong stones off the hatted heads of camel riders, just the way it should be for an eleven-year-old, or a 57-year-old for that matter. I pursue my habit (like I always have with my two girls) of trying to make a birdo and a botanist out of him, by offering him money - "I'll give you $10 for that bird Tommy." Eventually youth's retentive memory wins out, and I lose money. Then I hang in a 'double-or-nothing' with a tricky one, and get my money back - sometimes.

One afternoon, we came across a large Mulga flat that was over a kilometre in length. The very robust trees, more than ten metres in height, and some other factors, suggested that water would lie here for long periods, after heavy rain. There was also a good diversity of vegetation. We had almost travelled the length of this flat, when we came across three old Aboriginal Wurlies, consisting of Mulga framework. One of them was in quite a good state of repair, and could easily have taken the light thatching vegetation, required to complete the shelter.

These Wurlies would have last been used, prior to the clearing of Aboriginal people from the Great Victoria Desert, before the atom bomb tests in the 1950s. Dead Mulga branches will last for well over one hundred years, (fence posts) in the same ground that it naturally occurs. These Wurlies appeared to be very old, and certainly were our main point of interest for this day.

The dreaded Gyrostemon or 'gyro' is getting thicker. As a matter of fact, I have never seen it so thick. At some camps, we have to knock down and burn bushes, in order to let the camels feed relatively safely. On this evening, Spitta notices that his little Streaky is looking a bit off-colour. He hooshed down and looked bad, and Spitta ended up sitting up with him all night. He put a blanket on him, and gave him some gear to hopefully make him get rid of the suspected poison. Next morning Streaky is laying over on his side, and is obviously on his way out.

We headed off, leaving Spitta and Darren with Streaky, just in case, by some miracle he came good. However, as we were having lunch, Stubbie barks, and the two appear with only one camel. Streaky died only half an hour after we left. Spitta is a tough, rough diamond of a bloke, but has a heart as soft as butter. This really affected him, and he knew how his family were going to feel, having raised it from a calf; he rang them on the SAT phone and broke the news. I always look upon my camels as work animals, but you can't divorce yourself from your feelings towards them. They are truly loving gentle giants, and anyone that works them could not be unaffected by losing one. Several days later, something happened that ended sadly. I had a new cow camel, about ten years old, called Darky, a very sweet and gentle camel that mystified me, by not working to her full potential, and she kept hanging back on her lead rope. As a matter of fact she had bludged on the whole trip. This morning we were out shepherding, when Luke yelled out, "come over here." Darky was down on her side, and she was giving birth. She was not supposed to be in calf, but here it was. Quite often, it's very difficult to tell, and she sure sprung this one on us. In a matter of minutes, a dead bull calf was born prematurely. We cleaned up Darky as best we could, and I decided to have a day off, to give her a chance to recover. I was very annoyed about this, having paid plenty for her, but just as concerned now for her to get over it, with still ten days of hard trekking to go.

We got under away at one o'clock, with Darky walking along, but not happily, so we ended up leading her separately with a bit more success. Luke and Darren took it in turns, ending up at camp half an hour later than the string.

Author's note: This incident has a sad ending. Darky finished the expedition and seemed to be improving, with next to no loading. During the trip back to the Flinders Ranges, she appeared to be O.K. The last I saw of her at my Blinman Camel Farm, she was a camel on the mend. Twenty-four hours later, one of the local station blokes phoned me, telling me that she was down on her side. I kept in touch by phone for half a day, with her condition being constantly monitored. Then, judging by the reports, I reluctantly had to ask one of the blokes to put her down. Despite all our care, she must have developed an infection. I felt badly about that for a long time to come.

Lunches were always a favourite part of the day. We would find a shady situation (always easy in this desert, with big Marble Gums a favourite). We would spread a big four metre by four metre tarpaulin, and sit the two lunch-boxes upon it. While the billy boiled, the bread or damper is spread, and lunch of the day is cut up and put out. Quite often, sandwiches were made by a few volunteers or you could make your own, followed by cake or muesli bars and fruit. A look around, pack up, swap riders and we are off, usually within an hour of stopping.

Around half past four, I would get a GPS reading, and if we had knocked off the required distance, I would ride ahead, sometimes a kilometre or more, to find the best camel camp available. Looking firstly for suitable camel feed, with no or little Gyrostemon, and lastly a nice, aesthetic and interesting place.

In the latter part of this leg, we were encountering quite a lot of large Kurrajong trees (*Brachychiton*). Very often this was the only good camel feed around, and Darren Wallace (he and Fiona run a horticulture business in Melbourne) would often be seen in the top of a Kurrajong, cutting scrub with the machete, while the camels milled around underneath. Of late, you could sometimes see a Frisbee in action, saying something for the energy of this (some of them) crew. Some of them were already fit when they arrived, like Fiona, who does body building for a hobby, and loading pack bags every day kept her in condition. Others took a week or so to become fitness machines, but when they do, life takes on a new dimension.

Just when we thought we had shot our last feral camel, another bull is upon us as we are loading up, only three days from the finish. Spitta and I run out with rifles, and after the usual attempt to scare it off, I shoot it with my large bore, .375 Winchester carbine. One school of thought suggests that it is just getting rid of one member, of another slowly expanding feral animal population, but I can never rid myself of a deep melancholy, each time I have to destroy such a huge fine animal; definitely getting softer as I get older. This time I lost my bush knife as I ran after the camel, and carefully backtracked myself through the sand, scrub and spinifex; relief when I find it. It was hand made by Steve Watkins, a cameleer, from an old wagon spring that I found at Blinman, with a Wadi (*Acacia Puce*) handle, the world's heaviest timber; a valuable tool of trade. Steve has made various gear and saddles for the business, over the years, but his knives are second to none.

It is Saturday night, and we are almost to the cattle country. It is a sort of concert night, as Stubbie and I do our gig, with me on the mouth organ, knocking out Waltzing Matilda, and Stubbie emulating Peter Allen, often jumping from knee to knee, howling like a little lost soul. There are several more individual performances, but the repertoires are pretty well exhausted. People are healthy and fit but are tiring, but with a great sense of satisfaction, I'm sure. Most of our traverse, particularly for the second half, has been through a tract of the Great Victoria Desert, previously unvisited by Europeans, apart from one of Len Beadell's abandoned roads and an oil shot-line that we crossed yesterday. Next day we converge on the old well and bulldozer-loading ramp. That is our destination for tomorrow's loading, and signals the end of another memorable camel expedition.

As a dramatic finale that night, we see strange unexplained lights in the northwest sky. They move around for several minutes, up and down, across and finally disappear. This desert still has some secrets.

About the Author

Rex Ellis was born in 1942 and lives with his wife, Patti, at their Murray River camel farm. Their rammed earth and native timber house is surrounded by old growth Mallee scrub and located on colourful cliffs overlooking the River Murray. From this semi desert base he operates short summer safaris by camel, boat or 4WD vehicle, and longer safaris throughout the outback of Australia in the winter.After jackerooing and overseeing on sheep stations for six years, he began his safari business in 1965, operating in many 'non tourist' areas.

In 1971 he led the first party of tourists to cross the Simpson Desert and subsequent trips to other deserts and tropical regions, such as; Cape York Peninsula, The Gulf Country and the Kimberley region. His regular 4WD 'bread and butter' trips were to the Nullarbor /Great Victoria Desert and Birdsville/Strzelecki Tracks, and Flinders Ranges. He purchased the Birdsville Pub in 1973, and for six years used it as a base for trips into the Simpson Desert. Inland boat safaris became a specialty of his , after making the first and only crossing of Lake Eyre by boat during the 1974 floods. Since then he has followed most of the inland's flooding rivers and continues to do so. In 1976 he pioneered long haul desert camel expeditions and has crossed all of the Australian deserts.

This continues along with regular Flinders Ranges Treks. All of his itineraries are nature based. The four books he has written describe many of these journeys. His first book *Bush Safari*, details his earliest and more unusual trips by vehicle, boat, and camel. *Mulga Madness* includes several unusual safaris, but its main focus is on hilarious incidents on the sleep stations, bush towns and safaris, as well as some outrageous practical jokes. *Outback By Camel*, gives a comprehensive account of contemporary travel in the outback of Australia. He has almost completed his fifth book, *Boats In The Desert.*

In between times he writes his books, plants native trees, and pursues his interest in wildlife, in particular, birds.

Ten Thousand Campfires is Rex Ellis's fourth book.

His first book was *Bush Safari*, in which he described his more spectacular earlier safaris by 4WD, boats, and camels. His second book, *Mulga Madness*, concentrated mostly on outback humour, particularly some outrageous practical jokes on the sheep stations and also on the safaris that Ellis was either directly involved in, or observed from close-up. His third book, *Outback By Camel*, gives a comprehensive account of contemporary travel by camel in outback Australia.

His new book, *Ten Thousand Campfires*, is a smorgasbord of his bush humour and his experience leading safaris in the Outback over a period of more years than he cares to remember. But he also gives hilarious accounts of the down-to-earth tourist safaris that he led in Europe, Africa and India.

The book is illustrated with many of the author's colourful photographs. Even better there are numerous cartoons drawn by South Australian Bushie, George Aldridge, a long-time mate of Ellis. Aldridge is particularly fond of taking the Mickey out of Rex Ellis, capturing his foibles, his eccentricity and his many embarrassing faux-pas with his safari guests and the passing wild life.

Rex Ellis is a great yarn-spinner in the best outback tradition. He has a knack of combining exotic adventure with some rib-tickling humour.

Books by
Rex Ellis

Ten Thousand Campfires

Boats in the Desert

Mulga Madness

Mopokes and Mirages